Suicide Widow

My life story of persevering through adversity, addiction, and abandonment.

Krystal Youngs

Table of Contents

Introduction

Chapter 1: Worst Days Ever

Chapter 2: Jason's Worst Days Ever

Chapter 3: The Beginning

Chapter 4: Adulting

Chapter 5: My So-Called Perfect Life

Chapter 6: The Blame Game

Chapter 7: Identity Crisis

Chapter 8: The Grieving Process

Chapter 9: Widow

Chapter 10: Moving Forward

Conclusion

Introduction

It was just another Sunday. It was relatively warm for February 28th and my daughter, Charley, and I played outside on the swing set and she rode around on her bike. She kept asking where Daddy was, and I told her that he was working and would be home soon. We did chores around the house and made sure everything was neat and tidy. However, something wasn't right. Something didn't feel right to me.

I went on with my day and made sure that all my wifely duties were done, and my husband would be coming home to a nice, clean house and all his work clothes and other laundry done. The sheets were washed, the end tables were dusted, the dishes were done, and the floor was vacuumed. I made biscuits and gravy for supper. I made the best biscuits and gravy according to my husband. I started texting my husband asking when he would be home to eat because it was starting to get cold.

I would pace the floors for several hours wondering what was going on. My heart was racing, and my palms were sweaty. At about 5:00 pm that evening, there was a knock at our door. It was a knock that would change my life forever.

Chapter 1:
Worst Days Ever

I didn't think much of it, but I do remember saying, "Why would he knock on the door? Why wouldn't he just come in? Why is he knocking on his own door?" I opened the door and there stood our town police chief and the pastor that married my husband and me. I looked at them and looked down. I knew. I remember thinking, "no, no, no, no, no!" I looked back up at them and they told me my husband, Chad Youngs had been found in Clinton County and that he was deceased. In that one second, I lost half my heart, half of my soul, half of me. The state of shock that I was in was unbearable and I did not know what to do. I started pacing around and holding my head. My mind was racing and my heart was pounding. "What is happening?" I would continually say to myself over and over.

I looked at Charley and didn't know what to do. I went outside to smoke a cigarette and I was met by Chad's best friend and coworker, who just hugged me. He had been called by the police chief and was told that I would need him as soon as he could get to town. I was uncertain of what to do at his point. I was in so much shock that all I could think to do was walk around and smoke cigarettes. Who was I supposed to call and how was I supposed to tell people that my husband was dead? The first person I called was my sister, even though I hadn't talked to her in a very long time due to some of our family issues. I didn't care, and I just knew that I needed my sister. I struggled to make phone calls that night, as no one could understand me. I didn't even know what I was saying or who I was saying it to because I was so shocked and so panic-stricken.

After that, I was in such a state of confusion and utter shock that I had no idea what was going on, who was at my house, what had happened, why it happened, or where it happened? I was clueless. I just knew that I was hurting, my husband was found dead and I didn't have a clue what to do. Everyone was hugging me and patting my back and Charley was very suspicious of what was going on and why there were so many people in the house. She was enjoying the attention though. People were going through my things and telling me what I needed to do and what I didn't need to do. I felt like my soul was dead. I felt like I was dead and was in a living hell. This was the night of February 28, 2016. Now, let me go back.

February 27, 2016:

I was in a funk already. My father had called me three days prior and told me that he was diagnosed with esophageal cancer. Chad and I were devastated because we already knew that Chad's dad was diagnosed with bone cancer a year prior and we were in for a world of stress and pain. We sulked for quite a while and we were shocked.

I, however, was so excited for this day because it was the day of the Polar Plunge and those who knew me, knew that I lived for the Polar Plunge and getting our team organized and dressed up every year. It was a thrill for me and I loved being able to raise money for Special Olympics. I was up early doing my make-up to look like "Batgirl" and Charley a mini "Batgirl." If you knew Chad and I, if there was a special event, it usually involved alcohol in some way or another. Well, every day usually involved alcohol in some way or another. We started drinking early that morning so that I could get a good buzz going before I jumped into the frigid waters of Lake Viking.

We completed the plunge and during it, some kid threw a rock and it hit Chad in the head. He was enraged! I have never seen him so mad over something, other than if you were to touch his knee without him knowing.

However, the night before we attended a benefit for an individual who had cancer and Chad got mad at me because he couldn't hear me when I said something. I yelled back at him what I had said, and he got even more mad at me. He was very angry this night also. I just didn't see it as a warning sign. After the plunge, we went home, drank some more, BBQ'ed, argued, drank some more, invited some of the county deputies over for supper, drank more, argued and then, Chad left. He left because of a Facebook message that said, "are you coming out, if you do, then I will" on my phone. Chad always checked my Facebook messenger to make sure I wasn't texting anyone that I shouldn't be. It was almost like I had to be babysat, but when I was under the influence of alcohol, I didn't take anyone's feelings into consideration other than my own and I needed a babysitter.

He messaged the sender of this message and asked how he would feel if he sent something like that to his wife. The guy played it off like it was not a big deal and basically just laughed at Chad. He then posted something on his Facebook page about how it was ridiculous that guys and girls couldn't be friends and hang out without someone getting upset. This was obviously directed at Chad and he did not take it well. After one of the biggest arguments that we had ever had, Chad left the house, so I couldn't. We were both crying and sobbing and didn't know how to mend our broken, crumbled souls.

This argument is and will be forever burned in my mind. The yelling, the screaming, and the crying will never ever leave my mind. He didn't want me to go out partying, especially after some guy had just messaged me and asked if I was coming out. The last vision I had of my husband was his back walking to his truck, getting in and driving away. He was wearing a Snap-On coat that he had gotten from my father for Christmas. He was wearing a green shirt, blue jeans, and his tennis shoes. That would be the last time I would ever get to see my husband. I became angry that he had in a way, abandoned me and left me to where I wasn't in control of the situation.

I left the house that evening as well, with Charley. I wanted to be in control and do what I wanted to do. A friend of mine and two others, who were sober, came over and picked me up, got Charley out of bed and we went to their duplex to continue to drink and talk about how our lives sucked. When Chad returned home from his drunken rage, I was nowhere to be found and neither was our daughter. I didn't return home that night. My alcohol and life of partying was more important than my family, than my husband and had consumed my life. It had consumed my whole entire life. My actions that night was more than one of just being a terrible wife and led my husband to believe that I was going to leave him even though I told him I was not.

My last phone conversation with Chad was just before midnight. We talked for 6 minutes. I don't remember saying much to him other than, "We will talk about this tomorrow." Chad did not ever want to go to bed angry and I was the one who could sleep no matter what was going on. I wanted my brain to process whatever happened and then go back and analyze it the next day. I would drink and party until the wee hours of the morning not knowing the nightmare that I was about to call my life.

February 28, 2016:

Hungover and miserable, I came back home around 9 am. My friend's car was left at my house, so I took her back to my house to get her car. I knew something was not right because he never came home. His truck was not in the driveway and it was not in the garage. The grill was still outside, and nothing had been touched. It was just exactly the way it was the night before. The only difference was that his wedding ring and firefighter necklace that I had bought for him was on the kitchen counter by the coffee pot. He left them there after he came home and realized that I was not there. My friend saw this also and told me I should go with her and I told her no. I told her something was not right.

I called him, and it went to voicemail. I text him, and he would not text me back. In my mind, I thought he was somewhere cooling down because he was so angry from the night before. One time that day, and only once, I had a thought. It was a thought that would haunt me the rest of the day. I went into our room and looked for his Bersa .380 and the Glock, just to make sure. They were both the guns that he carried on a normal basis and they were both there. A weight was lifted from my chest. The gun that he did use he had gotten out of his gun safe that was in our basement.

Later that afternoon, I started to get angrier and angrier. I didn't understand why he wasn't messaging me back or why he hadn't been on Facebook for so many hours. I started to panic and started texting people to see if they had seen Chad's truck or seen Chad because I didn't know where he was. They would ask if everything was ok and I replied that it was however, it was not. It was not ok at all. This was the night I found out that my husband was found deceased after a self-inflicted gunshot wound to the head. He was found in the middle of a field.

I told everyone in my house that night that there was a 30 pack of Bud Light in the refrigerator and liquor bottles in the cabinet. I told everyone that I wanted them removed from my home because I was never going to drink again in my life. That was what killed my husband and I didn't want any part of it. That wouldn't last long, though. Someone also came up with the bright idea to remove all of Chad's arsenal of firearms from our house. I was not smart enough to figure out how to use a gun, let alone use it to kill myself. Them being taken elsewhere turned out to be a nightmare. Hindsight is 20/20.

February 29, 2016:

I woke up and called my doctor. I wanted something to help me sleep and not make me feel any pain whatsoever. I sat in my chair and sobbed and sobbed all day long. I stared at the wall and people continued to trickle in and out of my home all day long. My father came to visit me early that morning and was there to support me all day. All I knew was that apparently my husband was dead and all I could think of was our argument the night before. That damn argument.

Two deputies from the Clinton County Sheriff's Office came over and questioned me, even though I had no idea what was going on. At this time, I did not even know why he was deceased, where he was in Clinton County or where he shot himself. We went to my daughter's bedroom and they questioned me. I remember they told me that they had talked to several people and that Chad and I were good people. I replied, "Well, that's good." They knew I worked at the Sheriff's Office at one time and Chad worked for the city. They knew that we didn't have any enemies and that we were financially stable. It kind of creeped me out, really, but, I know now that it is protocol and what they must do. They asked if I knew what a motive for his suicide would be and I stated that he was depressed, drunk and we were fighting. What was the motive? What was the catalyst? I never saw this coming in a million years.

I had to start thinking about funeral arrangements. How in the world do you arrange a funeral when you are in a state of shock and can't even comprehend life? How do you know how to plan a funeral for your husband when it was so unexpected? How am I supposed to do this when my brain is a fog? At the funeral home, when we were doing the funeral planning, I could not even remember what day our anniversary was. I can honestly say this was the hardest thing I ever had to do in my life. Take a moment and think about how you would feel if you were in my shoes, in that moment of time. How would you feel having to quickly plan a funeral for the person that you love the most in the world and that you were supposed to live the rest of your life with?

I was asked where I wanted Chad buried, what I wanted him to wear, and what I wanted his headstone to look like. I was asked if I wanted to have a headstone with my name on it also. I was told, "Well, Krystal, you are so young and you will get remarried so you don't need a double headstone." I was instantly pissed. What do you mean I am going to remarry? My husband just died, and you are telling me I am going to remarry? I was unable to think clearly.

March 1-3rd, 2016:

I really do not remember anything from the 1st and the 2nd except that I did not eat, and I did not feel anything. The trauma that had just happened was disastrous. I sat in my chair and rocked continuously hoping that everything would go away, and I would not be in pain anymore. I would think to myself, "Maybe if I just sit here long enough then Chad will come walking through the front door and everything will be back to normal." I went on a ride with one of our local law enforcement officers to clear my mind. He told me that Chad was shot in the mouth. I didn't ask any more questions and started to sulk on the fact that my husband took his own life. I didn't even want to imagine in my head what he looked like.

Chad's visitation was on the 3rd of March. We had to have it held at the same church that we were married in because we knew it would be so big that it couldn't be held at the funeral home. I was not very happy about this, but we had no other choice. I walked up to his casket in the funeral home on the morning of March 3rd. This was my final time that I got to spend with Chad by myself, even though I couldn't see him or touch him. I remember not being able to hear anything but my own deep breaths as I walked slowly up to the red, shiny casket that held the deceased body of my beloved husband.

I was in a room all alone with my dead 37-year-old husband in a casket. A casket that I had to pick out myself. I don't remember what I said or if I even said anything, but I was broken. I didn't see his lifeless body because I didn't want to. On this day, the funeral director advised me that Chad's death was ruled undetermined. "What? Why? What does that mean," I said? He said in the 25 years he had been a funeral director that he had never seen anything like this. I was told he was shot in the back of the head. I was so confused. Who shoots themselves in the back of the head? Confusion continued to mount. As a sat there and stared at his red casket, I could literally feel my heart break in my chest. I felt like I was having a heart attack only it was from a broken heart. I laid on the floor in front of that casket and bawled my eyes out because I did not understand. It was the ugly crying that people do when they have snot running out of their nose and teardrops all over my face and shirt. I kept asking Chad, "WHY?" I kept asking God, "WHY?" I was about to be forced kicking and screaming into a life that I didn't want to have to live. I remember seeing his casket at the visitation in the same spot that my grandfather passed me off to him on March 27, 2010. It was in the exact same spot. My heart broke into a million pieces and I didn't understand why I had to go through this.

I became angry with God at this time and lost my faith altogether. His visitation lasted forever and ever and ever. There were so many people in and out. The line was all the way outside and around the building. If Chad could have seen all the people there, maybe it would have appeased him to know that he was loved. I am not much of a hugger, but I had to hug so many people that evening. When it was all said and done, I wanted to take a bath in germ-x. I was so tired and exhausted but had to prepare for the next day. The next day would be a day of hell that I would have to conquer on my own.

March 4th, 2016:

I am not going to lie, but this day was a major blur. I don't even remember if it was cold or warm, sunny or cloudy. I cried so much this day I could have sworn I was dehydrated from crying so much. Is that possible? I cried and cried and cried and cried. The ceremony was good, I think. I think it was what Chad would have wanted if he could have planned his own funeral. I picked the music that he would have wanted and made sure his favorite pictures were a part of his slideshow. I went through numerous pictures to figure out which ones were worthy of being shown at the funeral. That made it more real. I would have to stare at Chad's face in all the pictures but never be able to touch it ever again. I sat in the front row, dressed in black. A 28-year-old widow all dressed in black. I still stared at the casket in disbelief. I could picture in my mind my grandfather passing me off to Chad on our wedding day and how happy we both were. What happened??

I remember hearing myself sobbing while the sheriff sang "I Can Only Imagine." The sheriff sang at our wedding also. Why did there have to be so many similarities between our wedding and his funeral? I couldn't tell you who was there, or who was not, without looking at the guestbook. I don't remember much about going to the cemetery other than the pictures that I saw. My sister drove me out there in my car. I followed the vehicle carrying my husband's body that was getting ready to be placed into the ground forever.

He was dressed in his fire uniform that the firefighters wore at funerals. He always looked so good in it and I knew he would want to be in it forever. The funeral was over, and everyone went home. I was stuck in our house, with all our memories, all alone. I was stuck in a nightmare forever. I didn't know how I was going to continue with my life or how I was going to deal with everything that had to be done.

Now that you got to hear my side of the story, I would like to share with you, Chad's brother, Jason Youngs' story of those terribly excruciatingly painful days.

Chapter 2:
Jason's Worst Days Ever

Just another day in February

"On 02/27/2016, at 2120 hours, incoming text message "love you brother", I love you too. Then two solid tones in my ear, vehicle fire at Casey's general store, show me en route. I arrive, to the vehicle ablaze, I clear the building and ensure the emergency cutoff to the pumps is activated. Moments later the fire is out, and we stand in awe over the destruction it has caused. I point out to my partner the steering wheel of the vehicle and how it was made of magnesium, my brother taught me that. I took pictures to send to Chad later on.

02/28/2016, at approximately 0020 hours, burglary in progress homeowner fighting suspect inside the home, show me en-route. Partner and I arrive, to the residence to see the homeowner with the suspect pinned to the ground in the front yard. I have less lethal my partner has lethal, I give commands, yet he pretends as if we are not even there. I yell Taser Taser, he complies and is taken into custody. I go home and go to sleep, something doesn't feel right, it was a busy night so maybe that's it. Little did I know my whole world had stopped and I would never talk to Chad again.

02/28/2016 at 1700 hours, I'm on my way to work and get to that intersection that I always called Chad at. No ring, straight to voicemail. That is odd, I don't think Chad's phone has ever gone straight to voicemail and I call him every day. I tried two more times and got the same results, so I try Krystal, straight to voicemail too. I call up a friend to chat for a bit, he is a Police Officer too. He isn't up to much but says the Sheriff's Office is right outside his city limits working a suicide. That's horrible man, glad it was in County though, so you don't have to work it, "yeah gunshot wound to the head".

Dressed for work, checks complete, on my first call. Returned to my patrol vehicle to see a message from Krystal to call her "ASAI". I think to myself, jokingly "call you ASAI?" I knew what she meant but still found it comical. Little did I know how much distress she was in when she sent that message. I stand in headquarters and call her, she's crying, and I cannot understand anything she is saying. I finally get something out of her, "he's gone, Chad is gone!" Well, where the hell is he? was my reply. "He's in Clinton County, he's gone" What the hell is he doing in Clinton County? Tell him to come home." And then I remember my conversation with my friend earlier. "yeah gunshot wound to the head".

I'm going to stop here for a moment. Now I have received a lot of negativity because I was able to make this connection so quickly and believed that it was, what it actually was. If you think for a second that Chad was not capable of doing such a thing then you did not really know who Chad was. Never in a million years did I think he would ever do such a thing but, to say that he wasn't capable of it is just ridiculous.

What!? This draws the attention of my partner, he knows, he doesn't know what, but he knows. He gets on the radio, calls for our Sergeant to respond to Headquarters and takes me out of service. I fall to my knees and he kneels beside me, my brother is dead, he's dead. My partner starts to console me and begins to remove my gear. I remove my firearm, make it safe and hand it to him. I had to make sure that he knew I wasn't going to hurt myself, he knew what my brother meant to me. He takes off my vest, removes my duty belt, then just holds me. Though I am in a pile on the office floor, I instantly go into a spin and my first thought is that I have to stop the notification to my mother. No one but me is allowed to bring that kind of news to my mother, no one. I go into cop mode and bark orders, call Clay County and stop the notification to my mother, call Clinton County and get my official notification, I'll call Daviess County to make sure I am understanding this right. I am sorry I do not remember who answered the phone in Daviess County that evening. I know how incredibly difficult it must have been hearing my voice. But, she confirmed my worst fear, it is real, it is all real.

I don't know what to do, I want to get in my patrol car and scream down the interstate to make sure I am the first one to tell my mother and sister. My Sergeant makes arrangements to get me home and calls in fellow Officers to drive me and my car home. Though it was his responsibility, for this kind act, I will forever be in debt. I called the one person I knew was strong enough to help me through. She has been my rock through my struggles in life and I knew I could count on her. She answers the phone as she always did when I called. I'm sorry I have to tell you this on the phone, but I need you to meet me at mom's house.

Julie calls me before I am able to get home, "hey have you talked to Chad? His phone is going straight to voicemail" No I haven't, why what's up? Julie reads me like a book and knows bad news is coming. I will be there in a minute, let me talk to mom. Mom picks up and is her cheerful self. Little does she know, I am about to bring her the most horrific news she has ever received in her life. Hey, mom, I need you to be strong for Julie please, I will be there in a minute. She's a mother and she kicks right in to support mode without asking questions, thank god she didn't ask questions.

I arrive at mom's house with my support in tow, mom and Julie are waiting on the front step. I ask Julie to go inside so we can talk and she strikes me, "tell me now". Mind you this is the hardest thing I have ever had to do, I have given death notifications at work but this did not compare. I try to remain in cop mode but when it is time to speak, the tactfulness that I am known for is nowhere to be found. All I can say is, Chad shot himself. The screams are like none I have ever heard before. "Is he ok?". He is dead.

I slept next to my mother in bed that night. Trying to understand what it must be like to lose a child! But who am I kidding, no one in that house slept that night. I had to get to Krystal and Charley, they needed me. See Chad and I knew that our families would be taken care of in the event of a tragedy, he and I counted on one another for that.

02/29/2016, why didn't you do it on this day it only comes around every four years? Wait, why didn't you call me before you did it at all? Were you ashamed? Did you think I would catch it in your voice and try to stop you? Did you think that I would be able to talk you out of it? Or did you know that I was at work and knew that others were counting on me? You should have just called man. What I Would give to hear your voice again. I pull up to your house and I am on fire inside. I walk inside and embrace Krystal, I did not cry though. Krystal didn't have time for me to be crying, she needed a rock. I will be that rock, forever, no matter what.

Three days in March.

Turns out I was becoming everybody's rock. I do my crying in my pillow at night, no one has time for me to be weak, they need me. The arrangements, the visitation, and the funeral, Chad would not want me to cry. But inside I am dying, I shed ten tears to every one tear I see fall from someone else's face. I've always done things to be like my brother, how do I not take my own life now too? This is a visualization that I still deal with daily. I ask myself how I will not give up when I turn his age. I am falling into a deep depression, so deep that you don't even realize it is there because I have internalized everything. The overwhelming rage I feel inside the sadness, the heartbreak. "Jason, don't take this wrong, but I would have suspected you to take your own life before Chad" Yeah, that was said. I am initially overly offended by this statement. You actually think I am not man enough to take care of myself? You think I don't know what to do and where to go for help? You think I am afraid to get help or to say I have a problem? But then I carried my brother's casket, the heaviest thing I have ever carried. I began to doubt myself and my abilities to cope. As a recovering alcoholic, I was absolutely terrified. I have myself convinced at this point that I will return to drinking and ultimately take my own life in a drunken stupor.

I am a Crisis Intervention Officer, I talk people out of killing themselves, I get people the help they so desperately need. How did I not see the signs in my own brother? How was I so oblivious to what was right in front of me all these years? The truth is, I did know, I did see, and I did try to stop it. Never once did I think he would commit, but I knew he was in pain, I knew he had problems. I am going to toot my own horn here for a minute. I was the only person to ever tell Chad and Krystal that they had a drinking problem. I was the only person that told them they needed to quit drinking. But Chad was Chad, he could handle it in my eyes, so it wasn't really a problem. My concern was mostly in Krystal, I told Chad he needed to take care of her and get her the help she needed to quit. He acknowledged and agreed, he would take care of it. But he had the problem too and there was nothing he could do.

So here is the elephant in the room, I have thought numerous times of taking my own life, more than you could ever imagine. I have had those nasty thoughts for most of my life. I sought out the help I needed, I was able to overcome those nasty thoughts. "What about your kids Jason?" What about them? Do you seriously believe that when someone is in such a dark place they are thinking about the reasons to be alive? Suicide is selfish, and I don't mean that in a bad way at all. It is truly about the person having the thoughts. When they believe that their loved ones will be better off without them. What people fail to understand is that Chad was under the influence. Alcohol is a depressant and when you are down, it drags you down further. I beg of you to please believe that alcohol killed Chad, not a gun, not himself.

From the second I heard the news, I knew what had happened. People have said that Krystal hired someone to do it, that Krystal asked for a divorce and it was more than he could bear, and my favorite one, Krystal and I were having an affair and Chad was on his way to Kearney to beat me up when he just couldn't stand the thought and pulled over to end it all. Really? No one wanted to believe that he could do this to himself and thought that I was crazy for believing it. Please people, I deal with this kind of thing for a living, I am not a child anymore and have experienced quite a bit more than most people think. Everyone grieves differently, and I understand that I never forced my beliefs on anyone but have slowly observed people coming to the realization that I was right. You don't have to like it, you just have to live with it, in your own way.

Now anyone who knows me knows how important Chad was in my life. He was my brother, best friend and at times my father. He knew every detail of my life and carried me through the hardest times. The thought of living without him is almost more than I could handle at times. You have to understand that it is ok to talk about your problems, it is ok to ask for help. We have to kill the stigma, we have to stick together, and we have to love one another.

Carry on.

Two weeks had passed, and I had watched my family crumble to a pile of rubble before my own feet. I was off from work and began to find little purpose in life. My depression was getting worse and insomnia wasn't making things any easier. I remember Chad always telling me that there was somebody out there worse off than me. Though at the time this was hard to see, I had to consider that it had to be true. So what was I to do with this information? Well, I went back to work. The faces of my coworkers when I returned was priceless. They just could not believe I was already back to work, having only missed seven shifts. I was even asked, "What the hell are you doing here?" The answer was simple, I could come back to work, or I could sit in my head at home. At the time, my head was a scary damn place and I had no desire to be alone with it. Someone was worse off than I was and maybe I could help them.

I have used my unfortunate new found experience many times at work. I have spoken to thousands of people on the subject matter. I have decided that I have to take what I know and bestow it upon others, with the hopes that they realize someone cares. I feel I bare a great deal of responsibility to pass along what I now know. This is my way of healing and moving on. This must be talked about, this must stop.

Who was he?

Have you ever met someone that could change your mood, just by seeing them? Someone that wouldn't judge you when you did something they disagreed with? What about someone who would drop everything they were doing to rush to your side when you needed them most?

Have you ever wanted to be just like someone because they seemed to be impenetrable? They seemed like no matter what got thrown their way, they would rise on the side of victory? Someone who could listen to your deepest secrets and never speak them to anyone?

Can you imagine someone who will give you everything they own so that you can make it through? What about someone who can pass knowledge along and not even realize they've done so?

Think about someone who possesses so much love that they don't know where to place it all. A person that can do all of these things yet be in so much pain. A person that will never let you know how hurt they are, even when they know it will make them feel better.

Do you know a person like this? Maybe you've read about this person or seen them in pictures. Maybe you've stood beside a person like this and accidentally took it for granted. Have you ever met a real hero or even know what a real hero is?

Have you ever lost this person? Did you stare at a wall until your vision was so blurry, you swear that person was standing in front of you? Have you cried yourself to sleep every night because you blame yourself? Have you ever wanted to talk to this person just one more time to tell them how sorry you are? Have you ever awaken, drenched in sweat because you saw them in your dreams?

Have you ever taken this person for granted? Have you ever been so blind and self-centered that you failed to realize their pain? Have you ever let someone down and never apologized for doing so? Have you ever brushed someone aside because you had better things to do?

I know of this person. I have met this person. I have loved this person. I have trusted this person. I have counted on this person. I have looked up to and wanted to be just like this person. I have laughed and cried with this person. I have taken this person for granted. I have let this person down. I have mourned this person. Been mad at this person. Cussed this person. I have cried for this person. Seen this person in my dreams. I would DIE for this person!

This person, so kind and gentle. So strong and monumental. This person, so courageous it's contagious. This person, so ambitious and affectionate. So considerate and benevolent. This person, intuitive, gregarious, exuberant, passionate, reliable, sincere. and sympathetic. I could spend hours using words to describe this person.

This person is my hero, my strength, my best friend. This person is my brother. This person is Chad Youngs."

Hard to read, isn't it? I wonder if people now realize that when they were telling others of what they thought happened and why they thought it happened that they realize that there was a whole family that was suffering through it all. A family that struggled themselves to move forward and stay alive. A family, not just me, that was hurt by everyone's negativity and judgment. I would not wish that upon my worst enemy. The pain, anguish, hurt, sorrow, disgust, and broken hearts that we would deal with is something I would not wish on anyone. Although it is very nice and uplifting when people tell me how strong I am and don't know how I have made it through, there is one thing that they don't notice. I was not given a choice. I had to be strong, I had to move forward, and I had to keep going no matter what. We all had to, and we still have to be strong to this day. We had to learn a new normal and a new way to live life.

Chapter 3:
The Beginning

My mother was portrayed as a wild child and was out running around the town when she was 12 or 13 years old. She started using drugs and alcohol at an early age. She coped with her feelings by using drugs and alcohol as an outlet. She ran away from home several times also. In one instance she became pregnant, with my sister, and my grandfather, which was my mother's father, had to go get her and bring her back. She was pregnant with my older sister, Brandi. Brandi's dad was nowhere to be found and never would be. Our grandparents were at the hospital when Brandi was born, and they would take her home and raise her as their own.

My mother lived at home with them for a while. When Brandi was 3 months old and my mother was 18, she would leave home again. My grandparents then went to court and got guardianship of Brandi. Three years later, she would become pregnant with me.

My mother had a best friend that she was very close to. She lived with her for a while when she was pregnant with me. Her friend was diagnosed with cancer when she was 16 years old and then it went into remission, for a while. She had a daughter that was the same age as Brandi and then was pregnant with her next daughter when my mother was pregnant with me. She gave birth to her daughter and then passed away a few weeks later. My mother was devasted and was faced with a terrible trauma to deal with. She had to witness her best friend unresponsive, unrecognizable, bloated and hooked to many machines. My mother shared stories with me of her friend telling her that she knew she was dying. She then had to witness her best friend deceased and would never be able to see her again.

My mother and father met through mutual friends. They had a lot of good times together from what I have been told. I was born on May 12, 1987, at Truman Medical Center in Kansas City, Missouri. My mother and father were never married and dated for about 3 years. My father was born into a very good family. He started using marijuana when he was 8th grade. I am assuming that substance use is what brought my parents together. I would relate to this in the future.

My grandparents set my mother up with an apartment in for her to raise me, so they did not have to raise another grandchild. They got her set up with SNAP and other resources, so she would be set to raise me. This would not last for long though. I was told that I was left by my mother with the "babysitter" when I was a few months old. In her defense, she made a decision to leave me with someone who was able to take care of me because she was not at that time. My mother didn't know how to deal with the trauma that she had just experienced with losing her best friend to cancer and chose drugs and alcohol. She had just experienced death and the first death that she had ever experienced in her life. She was trying to self-medicate and numb the pain. She tried to raise me, but just couldn't kick the grief. My mother was lucky to have survived the trauma.

I completely understand now.

I knew this woman as the "babysitter" my whole life and never actually got the chance to ever meet her until later when I found her on Facebook. My father would come and visit while I was at this house on a weekly basis. He was also using drugs at the time and was unable to take care of me so, me being with the "babysitter" was ok with him also. All in all, I was probably right where I needed to be except I wasn't with my family. However, I developed a habit while I was there. I would literally bang my head on my pillow and sing to myself in order to fall asleep. I don't know why but it was the only way that I could get myself to sleep. Looking back, it seems silly, but I was self-soothing and trying to find a way to drown out background noise.

Why did they leave me? They were stuck in their addiction and didn't know what else to do. They had to abandon me in order to do what was best for me. My mother was dealing with her own trauma and didn't know how to cope with life. Much like I didn't after my husband died. The only difference, Charley was pretty well self-sufficient when I experienced my trauma and I was only an infant when my mother experienced hers. Ultimately, my mother did not want me to fail in life and wanted the best for me.

 I would stay with the babysitter until I was roughly 18 months old. My father would always take me out to see his girlfriend, who would eventually end up being my stepmother. My grandfather saw my mother at a gas station and asked her where I was. She hesitated. He asked again and asked if she had even seen me. He finally got out of her where I was, and he and my great-grandfather went to get me. She wanted me to be with my sister. My grandfather told me that I was screaming and crying. I was walking around the house wondering where my "mommy" was. The

My love for Brett Favre would be my trademark by the 6th grade. Everyone knew that I loved Brett Favre and the Green Bay Packers. I watched football with my uncle all the time and developed my love for football. He was more like my big brother, as he lived with us until he was in his late 20's. I moved from the North Platte School District in 6th grade. My grandparents tried to prevent Brandi and I from going down the same road as our mother. I went from a large class to a class of 8 students. I was 12 when I moved to Gilman City. We built a huge house in the country. It was a house that really should have been a bed and breakfast because it was so large. I am not complaining because I was living the dream. I had everything that I could ever want when it came to material things. I always dressed nicely except for when I went through a phase of wearing baggy jeans and baggy t-shirts and listening to heavy metal music daily.

I struggled in high school, not education wise, but socially wise. When I was in 7th grade, I started smoking marijuana. Is that a coincidence? I don't know why I started, I just was around people that did it, so I did. My grandparents would always use the phrase, "you are who you run with." They were right. The friends that I had would significantly impact my choices and behaviors for the rest of my high school years and beyond. I felt that ever since I moved there and started smoking marijuana that I would always be known as a "pothead." That period didn't last long, however. I didn't do it anymore in 8th grade and I met a friend of mine, who I still adore to this day, that explained to me how bad marijuana was and how I shouldn't do it. Obviously, I should have known this myself but didn't. He was a preacher's son, but he didn't show any judgment; he just tried to help me.

My class was full of boys and we had the occasional girl that would move in, but I was there from 7th grade on with those boys and they became my best friends. We went through so much together. When you grow up around that many boys they are obviously going to tell you every flaw that you have. I did blame them for my low self-esteem, but I know that they didn't have anyone else to pick on and I shouldn't have taken it as personally as I did. They used to tell me that my behind looked like two Christmas hams. That caused me to start taking weight loss pills in the 8th grade. My sister found them in my backpack and told me I was stupid, but I was very self-conscious.

My first suicide attempt was around this time. I had a UTI and a Kidney infection and was prescribed antibiotics. I took the whole bottle of antibiotics, but it did nothing but make me have a very high fever and become very sick. I survived and realized I still had a life to live so I kept going. I never knew much about suicide growing up because it wasn't something that was talked about. I don't even know how I found out that a person is actually capable of taking their own life. Apparently, sex education was more important to talk about with us in school. Our sex education class was a joke. We were told that if someone sleeps around it was like having a bunch of different people putting their foot in a shoe. Seriously? I will never forget when we were discussing abstinence and one of my classmates said,

"Abstinence? I gotta get me some of that!" It was a quote that will be remembered by us forever.

When I was a sophomore in high school, I started to change. I started to dress nicer and not wear JNCO jeans and baggy t-shirts. I started wearing fitted shirts, curling my hair and being well, more like my sister. I met a boy when I was a sophomore in high school that would end up being a huge part of my adolescent life. I would be cheering at basketball games and I always had my eye on him. I knew his name, but I did not know him. We had an assembly at our school and two other school districts were going to be there, so I knew that he was going to be there, since his school district would be there. I asked my sister to dress me that day and do my hair. I saw him walk up the stairs that day looking right at me and I looked right at him. I told my fellow male classmates that he stared at me and I was very excited. They were quick to tell me that he was probably looking at the person behind me or that I had something on my face. That boy would call me a few days later and ask me on a date. He would be a part of my life for the next 5 years.

I wasn't a very smart teenager, although I don't really think any of us are. Who wants to have wisdom as a teenager? What fun would that be? It is a learning process. I never really knew how to have a happy relationship. No one ever taught me the ins and outs of dating and how to be faithful and loving. Don't get me wrong, we were happy for a very long time but the older we got the more issues that came along. He cheated, I cheated, and we started to move our separate ways. We were together, we broke up, we were together, and we broke up over and over again. I think that is just part of it though. We were two good people but just weren't worth a damn together. However, our on and off again struggle would last for several more years. I would choose my friends and alcohol over him which caused several issues. This would be a trend that would continue into my adult life and do more harm than good.

Brandi, my sister, would struggle at this point in her life due to relationship issues. She attempted suicide by slitting her wrists with a box cutter. She would be admitted to the mental health unit, where I would go visit her. This would not be the first time that she attempted to cut her wrists, however. Chad informed me of many times that she would threaten suicide and go running through the timber with a box cutter. Chad would always run after her to save her and keep her from doing it.

I first met Chad Alan Youngs from hanging out with my sister and her husband at the time. Her husband at the time and Chad were distant cousins, as Chad's grandmother and his grandfather were brother and sister. Chad was married to his first wife when I first met him. I remember I had just received Homecoming Queen during my senior year of high school and I went to my sister's house the following day wearing my Homecoming crown. I was so excited about my accomplishment of winning Homecoming Queen, although to many it wouldn't have meant much. I did not know when I met Chad that he would turn out to be the love of my life. Obviously not when I was in high school because I was underage, and it would have been illegal.

I think back to all the fun times that we all had in high school and it instantly puts a smile on my face. Our junior year, the whole class decided to leave school at lunch, hop into my father's Tahoe that he let me borrow and take off for lunch without telling a soul. We all ended up getting ISS for a few days, but it was worth it. We may or may not have taken my father's Tahoe out to "booze cruise" one night and blown the speakers out also. After that, my father always gave me a minivan to drive. Thanks dad! Our senior year, we took two skip days which landed us all in ISS. Again, it was totally worth it. We spent our Senior Skip Day golfing and then went to the river and drank. We were all our own people and we all accepted each other for who we were. We didn't always get along, but we always had each other's backs.

I remember one evening, I was at home getting ready to go to bed and I heard a knock at my window on the second level of our two-story house. I didn't look out the window because I was freaked out at the time. Then, I got a phone call from a boy in my class. He stated he was outside on my roof and wanted me to come out because he had a ladder I could climb down. Little did he know; my grandfather had just gotten home from work and had taken the dogs out to go to the bathroom when he noticed the ladder. He came into my room with a handgun and asked who was on the roof because he had knocked it down. I, of course, lied and told him that I didn't know. The boy jumped off of the second story and back to his truck. My grandfather kept the ladder until I finally snuck it out to the boy a few months later when my grandfather was at work. I finally caved and told my grandfather who it was. He just laughed and has mentioned it every time that he comes across that boy.

Overall, I had a decent high school experience. I graduated third out of eight only by a few points. By all means and I know the other contender would agree, I should have been the class Salutatorian. I also want to mention one teacher who I know made a lasting impression in each of our lives. Mr. Vorthmann was our history teacher for a few years. He was also one of my bosses at the local grocery store when I worked there in high school. He wasn't like the other teachers and he was very relatable and one of the funniest people that I had ever met. I was very sad to see him go, but he has moved on in life and has become very successful.

I enjoyed going to high school at a smaller school and not having to deal with all the cliques. I didn't feel like we had that many cliques. In my class, we each had our own identity and we had to accept each other for who we were. I will never forget our senior trip to Orlando, Florida. It was a trip to remember for sure.

We stayed up late partying the night before we left and headed out around 5 am to get on the plane. I am not sure if we were still all under the influence or hungover, but we weren't very lively on the way to Florida. We had so much fun on the rides and trying different foods. We even got served non-virgin strawberry daiquiris at a Chinese restaurant. I also remember being outside of our hotel and staying up all night talking to a few of my fellow classmates. We would have some pretty interesting conversations in that parking lot. We would discuss our pasts and our futures and what we wanted for our lives. My father and mother attended my high school graduation. My father was under the influence of methamphetamine while at my graduation, though, and I was disgusted to say the least. I gave roses to my grandparents and my sister and not to my mother or father. I was still bitter. After we graduated, we all moved our separate ways and started adulting.

Chapter 4:
Adulting

When I turned 18, my grandparents received a letter in the mail that stated their guardianship over me had been terminated. That made me feel abandoned again because I technically did not have any parents. I was always referred to as a ward of the court. My grandparents never adopted me, which would help me when I went to college later on. Also, I do not believe that my father would have ever let that happen. When I graduated high school, my grandparents decided to sell their house and build a smaller one.

At that time, I had to find somewhere to live because there would not be enough room for me in the house they were renting at that time. I moved in with one of my friends and her family for that summer, as I was still working in that town and would stay there for a few years while going to school at Northwest Missouri State University for my undergrad. Her family took me in as their own and still claim me to this day. They will always be my adopted family. Although I was very, very, very ornery back in that day, they still treated me as one of their own.

The summer after I graduated high school involved a lot of alcohol. A lot of vodka, as it was my drink of choice. I was underage, so taking a few shots of vodka and then going out to a party would alleviate the need to bring any alcohol along and therefore, not end up with another MIP. Yes, that's right. I got a MIP while I was in high school because I had a bottle of vodka in my back seat. They took it from me and I had to do community service and then it was off my record. That didn't stop me from drinking though. You live, and you learn, I guess.

I would spend my summer working and drinking on the weekends with my friends. My high school boyfriend and I, that I mentioned earlier, were off and on still. He did not care for my friends, but I absolutely loved them. I also reverted back to marijuana back at this time. Not for long though, just for the summer before I started college. I was never around any other illegal drugs besides marijuana and I always look back and wonder if I would have tried anything else. I am sure I would have due to having an addictive personality. I would spend my nights blacking out from drinking too much and passing out on my friend's toilet. Vodka and I didn't get along really well. I did have a lot of fun that summer though, as I went to Rockfest, Worlds of Fun, and several drunken road trips. One that landed a friend of mine and myself in Iowa in the middle of nowhere. I didn't know what the future held for me at this time in my life. I was a lost soul. I was dealing with my issues the same way that both of my parents did, and I was running from something. I didn't know what I was running from though.

My college experience was interesting. Coming from a small high school and going to a school with thousands of people was very scary. I was very shy and didn't like to talk to a lot of people. I mainly hung out with people from the town that I went to high school at and people from the surrounding towns. I didn't drink a whole lot when I was in college except for on Thirsty Thursday when my friends and I would go out to a local bar or just hang out at a friend's house in town. It never failed that I always had an eight am class on Friday though. At this stage in my life, things were pretty quiet. I went back and forth from college during the week and then back home for the weekend. I was still dating my high school sweetheart off and on and I was focused on school and work. My second year at Northwest Missouri State University, my best friend and I had an apartment on campus with two other girls. We had a blast and were wild and crazy. I have video footage to prove that. My best friend and I would go to the coffee shop on campus and I would always get white hot chocolate and she would get a caramel macchiato. She was a very good influence on me. She was very level-headed, smart, and was determined. This was around the time that I got to know who Chad was.

I would see Chad off and on. He helped my grandfather move a few things from his storage unit from time to time. We often had parties at my sister and her husband's house. Chad got divorced and started to hang out more since he needed to be around people and not alone. Then, my best friend started dating Chad early in 2007 for a few months. I was still off and on with the boyfriend mentioned earlier, which happened to be my best friend's stepbrother.

My best friend and Chad ended up breaking up. I know she was devastated and I did feel bad for her because any break up is hard. I didn't feel like I was there for her as much as I should have been, but I was so wrapped up in my relationship drama that I wasn't paying attention to anything else. We endured some turmoil when she found out that Chad and I had been seeing each other but, as best friends do, we forgave and forgot. We both wanted each other to be happy and that was all that mattered.

I lived a nomadic lifestyle for a while at this point in my life. I had a better relationship with my mother at this time in my life and talked to her quite a bit. I would spend several weekends at her house and we would always go out and do something fun and go somewhere nice to eat. I enjoyed being around my mother and stepfather. I was able to talk to my mother about things in my past and got to hear her side of things on why she had abandoned me as an infant. I finally realized that she wasn't a bad person and her past did not define her. I realized that she was able to change and overcome her addictions, so I should be able to also.

After my second year at Northwest, I decided to transfer to Missouri Western State University and rent an apartment in a different town. I rented the apartment and my boyfriend ended up moving in with me, but I hid it from everyone. This did not last long at all, maybe a few months. He had just gotten out of being incarcerated for 120 days and we quickly found out that we could not live together and make it work. He would move out and move on and I would stay in the apartment all alone. Then, I struggled with drinking heavily again to numb my pain. Vodka again.

I would spend that spring and summer going to bars in St. Joseph and passing out in my friend's cars in the middle of the night. I would spend it mainly depressed and drunk. I was functional though and always made it to work and classes on time and somehow passed. I don't know how I really survived through all of it, but I did. This seems to be a pattern in my life.

My father would come to me during this period of my life. He came to me and told me that he wanted to be sober and was going to go to rehab. He apologized over and over but I kept telling him that it was ok, and I wanted him sober too. My grandparents were ok with my father at this time. I am not sure what the difference was between this time and when I was a child, but their view changed. My father checked into rehab and was able to remain clean and sober for the next 11 years.

Chapter 5:

My So-Called Perfect Life

The night that Chad and I "got together," he was an 18 pack deep. I had been drinking also because that is what I did. This was June 26, 2007. Chad went to get my cd's out of his truck after everyone had gone home and when he turned around, we were standing face to face. I would kiss my future husband for the first time this night. We would talk every single day since that first kiss. We continued to drink together, booze cruise, and do whatever involved drinking when we hung out. That seemed to be what brought us together. I say "got together" but it would take Chad several months to even ask me to be his girlfriend.

September of 2007, I was involved in a car accident that was very bad. I was drinking and driving and on my way home from a wedding reception. I had dropped my friend off and was headed to see Chad. I didn't make it but a mile outside of town I was in when I rolled my car and it ended up on its top in the middle of the highway. Chad was home with his son and heard the radio tones come out. He tried to call Brandi and her husband, who were at the bar and they had no signal, so he called the bar. My brother-in-law stayed with Chad's son, while Brandi and Chad headed my way. Brandi did state that this was the scariest truck ride that she had ever been on, as Chad's adrenaline was through the roof.

When they arrived, Brandi got out of the truck and was in the middle of the road making a dramatic scene and Chad was there talking to the cops. I knew the deputies there, as I had just started hanging out with Chad and he was close with them. I knew nothing about the process of a DWI or that I could even get a DWI. I blew over the legal limit, of course, I was only 20 so anything was over the legal limit. The highway patrolman eventually let Chad take me to his house. He gave me a ticket for a MIP and carless and imprudent driving. My thumb was ripped open and I had apparently lost my fake thumbnail, as well as my real thumbnail. Chad ended up taking me to the ER in Cameron to get me looked at and doctored up. I stayed the night with Chad, which was the first time I had ever stayed the night at his house. He took care of me that night and he continued to do so every single day after that.

After that, I lost my license and I was in a rut. I was still in my undergrad and had to make it to classes. Luckily, my best friend lived close by and we were able to carpool, as she would pick me up on her way to classes. I remember my sister's husband trying to get me to date Chad and I would say, "He's old and he has a kid!" I was only 20 years old at this time and Chad was 29. In October 2007, Chad purchased his first home, which would end up being our home. I stayed the night with him on October 31st and we drank beer out of crystal wine glasses and slept on the hide-a-bed. I also met his dad and uncle for the first time, as his uncle got his tractor stuck and his dad asked him to assist. I would stay with him a few times out of the week. I eventually started moving my things in. I got a larger TV for Christmas that year and brought it to his house, then my clothes, my tampons, and eventually me.

Our first fight was in December of 2007. It was right before the dreaded ice storm. I had been texting another guy that I knew from college and he found out. I was so upset with myself that I locked myself in his bathroom and eventually ran out into the night. Yes, I ran out in the middle of an ice storm, slipping and sliding all the way down the street. Chad went out on the ice storm that night and was gone for over 24 hours working. Once he had come home and gotten some sleep, we were able to discuss the situation. I remember yelling at Chad because he hadn't even called me his girlfriend and would only refer to me as a "friend." I told him that if I was worth having sex with then I should be worth being his girlfriend. I was pretty blunt about it, but he did understand. He was just scared to commit again, as he didn't want to get his heart broken. I understand that now.

We had another fight a few weeks later. We always hung out at the local mechanic shop and drank beer after work. We would stay there and drink, smoke, listen to music and talk about life with the other. Chad received the nickname "fish hook" and I received the name "Krystal the Sex Pistol." I don't know why, that is just what they called me. Chad had gotten mad at me again and left the shop one night. Of course, I still didn't have my license at this time and had the owner of the shop and a few others take me back to my apartment. Chad continually called wondering where we all went and why I wasn't going to his house. I told him I was going back to my apartment.

Shortly after arriving at my apartment, Chad walked through the door. I should note that Chad told me he was singing "I Can't Fight This Feeling" by REO Speedwagon on the way to my apartment. The first thing he said to me was, "Will you be my girlfriend?" I was in shock but quickly said yes. We packed up and we went back to our "home." Chad always told me that he never wanted to date or especially get married ever again. He told me that I would push just a little bit and then let off. He said when I let off was when he knew that he wanted to be with me. The feeling was mutual.

Chad and I continued to drink off and on. By this time, it was early 2008. I had to take SATOP to get my license back and after SATOP, I came home and told Chad that I wanted to stop drinking. Chad was ok with it and quit with me. We quit cold turkey. We would drink the occasional Busch NA if we went anywhere to feel like we fit in, but we were able to live our lives sober for the next 2 years with absolutely no issues in our relationship. We were that disgustingly happy couple that never fought and was so in love. We were always together and never doing anything that involved us being apart. We were that cute couple in the shopping mall that was holding hands and blowing kisses at each other. I absolutely loved it and was so in love with Chad. I had never felt that way about anyone before. He made me feel so special. I never ever had to get jealous or worry about him cheating on me. He was the most faithful man I ever met.

Chad used to do a lot of side jobs for people. He was always about helping everyone. We used to do a lot of tree jobs together. We worked as a team. He would cut, and I would drag the brush to the trailer. We worked in the heat, the rain, and the snow. This is when I bought my first pair of Muck boots. Chad enjoyed it, even though it was really hard work. I enjoyed being his sidekick and being able to help him make money.

Chad was a very, unique man. He never once raised his voice at me. He never once called me any derogatory names. He never once laid a hand on me. He never once disrespected me in any way. I had literally found my prince charming. I started working part-time for the Sheriff's Office starting in June of 2008. Chad had gotten me the job through one of his friends despite my past legal issues. We were not drinking at the time and the current sheriff had faith that I wasn't going to mess up. I didn't. I loved that job. I had so much fun with my coworkers and even better, Chad could stop in to see me at any time during the day. We also got to spend our lunch breaks together. We loved it and things continued to get better for us. I was only working part-time, and he was working full time, but we were able to survive and be happy.

Marriage was brought up several times. I understood that Chad was scared to be hurt again and go through what he went through before. I understood that he was hesitant, and I did not push. I did not force him in any way to even want to get married to me. It just happened. In December of 2008, Chad and I picked out our wedding rings. We bought them in advance, but Chad always told me that I would not know when he was going to propose. We were ready to embark on our journey of marriage but wanted it to be perfect. I waited patiently for him to propose and he finally did on my birthday in 2009. The day before, we were trying to save a friend of ours that was depressed and attempted suicide. Needless to say, we were exhausted.

The night of my birthday, I fell asleep on the couch in our living room. Chad put the ring on my right hand. Realized that he was wrong and had put it on the left hand and then woke me up. I was in disarray and did not know what was going on. I woke up and looked at my hand. Chad asked me to marry him and I screamed and said YES! I was going to be Mrs. Krystal Youngs for the rest of my life and I was so happy about it. I didn't want to wait over a year, so I decided to get married at the end of March, hoping the weather would be decent.

I graduated college from Missouri Western State University with a Bachelor's of Science in Elementary Education in December of 2009. In the fall of 2009, I completed my student teaching at Tri-County Elementary School. I asked to do my student teaching where I lived, and they turned me down. That is where my bitterness started. I will continue with that later on. My graduation was a happy day. My grandparents, mother, father, sister, mother in law and father in law were there. My father was sober, and I was so proud of him. I had accomplished something that no one in my immediate family had ever accomplished and I was so proud. I know Chad was ecstatic for me also. He wanted me to fulfill my dream of being an elementary school teacher. He came to a class party when I was student teaching and saw how much I enjoyed it and how much the kids enjoyed me. Unfortunately, finding a teaching job would be one of the hardest things I would ever have to go through. I applied everywhere. No one would hire me. I started to get a complex and wonder whether it was me and why I couldn't land a teaching job.

The wedding preparation began. I started deciding who was going to be in the wedding and who was going to help me with certain things and how I wanted everything to look. My favorite color is red, so I knew I wanted roses to be the flower in my bouquet and on corsages. I had several friends help me out over the next few months and I was thankful for that. Several friends offered to pay for many things and it helped tremendously. I was so excited to be Mrs. Youngs that nothing else really mattered. I was still only working part-time, and our income was limited. I didn't care what it took though, I wanted the wedding of my dreams with Chad and I just knew it was going to be my only wedding. We would get married in the First Christian Church. The pastor that married us went over a book with us to prepare us for marriage. We were ready to take on the world no matter what it took. We were ready to start the beginning of our whole lives together.

The months continued and then it was March 27, 2010. The most important day of my life was finally here. I was able to fulfill my perfect wedding with the perfect man. I was very stressed out on this day because number one, it was raining, and number two, I didn't know how the families were going to interact with each other. Chad's family had some turmoil which involved someone not wanting to be in the same room with his mother. Fortunately, there were no issues until the reception, which involved my family.

My mother did not want to stay at my reception because my father and his sister were in attendance and it made her feel uncomfortable. She left, and it caused me to become pretty upset. My mother and I did not speak for several years after this incident due to me feeling abandoned once again. Other than the family drama, our wedding was absolutely perfect.

It was everything that I had hoped and more. We were escorted out by the deputies and came into our reception with lights and sirens going.

One thing about our wedding that was different than our everyday life was that Chad and I had started drinking again. We drank at our bachelor/bachelorette parties because I thought it would be a good idea. I remember telling Chad, "Who gets married and doesn't drink at their reception?" Well, I am sure a lot of people do but that was my excuse to start drinking again. We had a joyous honeymoon and made a lot of new memories. was the first time Chad had been on a plane and the first time he had been to Universal Studios. It was my dream come true and I was with the man that I loved.

We returned home from the honeymoon and started our life as newlyweds. We were able to control our drinking and went out a lot with our friends. Everything was peachy. No fighting, no arguing, no lying, no manipulation, just pure heaven. We decided that we wanted to have a baby. I stopped taking my birth control in September and I didn't get pregnant. I told Chad his sperm was old and that was why I wasn't pregnant. He didn't appreciate that. The next month, October of 2010, I found out that I was pregnant. I didn't have health insurance, but I didn't care because I wanted to have Chad's baby and I wanted our family to be perfect. We were so excited that we could not hide it. I was at home and Chad came home for his lunch break one day. I decided to take the test. I peed on the stick and Chad took it from me. I was chasing him around our house trying to get him to give it to me and he refused. It finally showed up that I was pregnant. We were both speechless and didn't know what to do or who to call but we were super excited.

Then, in that same moment, my stepmother called and stated that my father had experienced a heart attack and was in the hospital. I was speechless once again but in a different way. I called him at the hospital and informed him that he was going to be a grandfather. I went to work that afternoon and it didn't take me long to let the cat out of the bag. I would be in for 9 months of fun. My pregnancy was not a bad one at all. I had some major heartburn and Charley liked to hang out in my ribs but other than that I could not complain. I should mention that my mother had no knowledge of me being pregnant or when our daughter was born. I would eventually stop being resentful and talk to my mother and make amends.

I knew that I had to do something regarding my health insurance. I couldn't get on Chad's because we would not be able to afford it. I was willing to pay full price for her if I had to. Luckily, I landed a job with health insurance two weeks before my due date. When I interviewed, they apparently did not know I was pregnant because when I told them that I would accept, but I was due in 2 weeks, they didn't know that I was pregnant. I went to work for a week and then took 7 weeks off for maternity leave.

My health insurance would come into effect on July 1, 2011, which was Charley's due date. I went into the hospital on June 30th after I was having some spotting. They kept me, and I went through 25 hours of labor altogether. After 23 hours, they decided to do a C-section because she did not want to come out. Charley Mae Youngs was born on July 1, 2011, at 4:09 pm. And the birth would be covered by my insurance, which was a blessing. The look on Chad's face when he first saw his daughter was a face of a proud, proud father. I will never forget seeing the joy and excitement on his face, as he held Charley in his arms for the first time.

Things continued to go well for Chad and me, as we were now newlyweds and new parents. Everything with Charley was fascinating to us, as Chad was getting to be a dad for the second time and my first time being a mother. Things remained normal for Chad and me until Charley was around 2 years old. That was when we started drinking, a lot. We would put her to bed and tie one on after she went to bed. Over the next two years, this would become considerably worse. I hated my job. I was fat, I had to work around criminals that stared at me all day long and I was constantly still trying to land a teaching position. I wanted out of that place. However, because I had a degree, I was able to promote after 6 months of being there. I received a very nice raise and was making close to the same as what Chad was. We didn't know what to do with all our income, but we did save quite a bit over the years. I was "tighter than bark on a tree" as Chad would say. He would always ask how much money we had, and my normal reply was, "we are broke."

In 2013, I had lost 30 pounds. I was feeling good about myself and I was making more friends at work. I still was not a fan of my job, after having to witness a black male masturbate to me and have been called everything but a white woman. It gave me a complex and I wouldn't let

Chad "talk dirty" to me because it was almost like PTSD from that God-forsaken place. Chad knew I was unhappy and always wished I could get a teaching job. I did apply for a para-professional position in the town we lived and was offered it for $11 an hour. I was making a considerable amount more than that at the time and I took it as a slap in the face. I couldn't take the pay cut. I promoted again, and I was actually happy with my job for once since I started working there. I was good at what I did, and I enjoyed going to work. Although, this is when things started to go south with my marriage and my life.

This is also when things started to go south with my relationship with Brandi. I believe at this time in our lives we were both lost souls and didn't have any guidance on how to do the right thing or what to do. We should have known better, as we were in our late 20's but we were never taught how to cope with life, thus our previous suicide attempts. We were never taught what we should do when we have relationship issues or get addicted to a substance. We wouldn't speak for several years due to Chad and I siding with her ex-husband, when we should have tried to mediate the situation instead. I regret that decision and regret ruining the relationship I had with my sister. However, after a long rough stretch and her being there for me when I absolutely needed her the most, we got our sisterhood back on track to where it needed to be.

Chad blamed my place of employment for our issues and wanted me out, however, I always told him we could not afford it. This is where life became messy and this is where my mind became messy. I made a lot of new friends, or so I thought they were friends at the time. We made a lot of new memories, but most of what we had in common, involved drinking. All the friends that Chad had before we got together were all settled down with children and would not go out and drink but once in a blue moon, so we didn't see them much at all.

Chad would drink when he came home from work and sit on his phone. I was left to take care of Charley, do everything around the house and take care of everything. Chad and I fought on a regular basis and we started drinking more and more. I became resentful towards him for him not helping me and being the husband that he was before. I lashed out in a way that I thought I would get even with him and started drinking myself.

We started drinking when Charley was awake and then eventually right when we just got home from work. We would spend our evenings in the kitchen, mainly sitting on the counter talking about life, whether it was good or bad. We would spend our evenings this way for several years. This may be too much information, but my interest in sex had gone down a whole lot also. That was a kick to Chad's ego, as he didn't feel like he was good enough. I tried medication, but nothing helped this. I didn't know why I had lost the sexual drive for my own husband, but it happened. I could not explain it to him of why I felt that way and it made him very upset and very angry. We had a very long dry spell before his passing.

Chad and I went back and forth of who wanted to quit drinking and when. He would want to and then I wouldn't.

I would want to and then he wouldn't, and it was this way for a long time. I went to a conference in the Bahamas and brought back some rum that was to die for. I noticed it evaporating so I started marking where it was at with a permanent marker. Chad was sneaking my rum when I wasn't around, and I called him on it. He got very mad at me and I told him if he wanted to get drunk get his own liquor because that was for special occasions. He didn't care because he was like me and just wanted to be drunk and it didn't matter how we got there.

Chad had just received a substantial raise with the city in January of 2016. He called me and told me he was going to buy a 30 pack and I asked why and he said he would be making $19 an hour now. He was so excited and felt that he was finally getting what he was worth out of the city. I was super excited too. I noticed a teaching opportunity for the spot of the teacher that I did my student teaching with and I applied for it. We would be fine financially, and I could now do what I initially wanted to do. I had Chad talked into moving to a different town because he could still work for the city, but he did not want to leave the volunteer fire district. That was a battle that we were fighting.

I would start to become selfish and self-centered. I would start to feel like I was invisible. This was farthest from the truth. I started hanging out with a friend that only wanted to hang out with me and not Chad. I thought it was ok and explained to Chad that we just needed "girl time." At that time, I had no interest in any other men anyway. My interest was completely about alcohol. I was in a relationship with alcohol and all that I cared about was getting drunk. We would have parties at our house and we would all get extremely drunk. I would go to the Mexican restaurant with my friends after work and have numerous margaritas. I would continuously go to the bar without him. That was just my life. Chad never questioned or accused. He would always be awake when I came home and would make sure that I was ok.

In early February 2016, Chad and I would open a retirement account that was for the both of us. His friend had told him it was a good thing and Chad wanted to be prepared for the future. He obviously wasn't thinking about taking his own life in a few weeks if we were just setting up a new retirement account to help us save for our future.

He also bought me a dozen roses for the first time this Valentine's Day. I would never let him spend the money, so he only usually bought me a few roses. I was home from work and Charley was at daycare. I was working on rearranging the office and I heard someone come in through the downstairs door, come up the stairs, set something on the table and go back down. I yelled, "Chad?" I heard nothing. I went in to the kitchen and found a dozen red roses on the table, a balloon and a flower for Charley. Chad soon text me and said he paid in cash, so I would never know how much he spent and that he loved me and Charley.

The remainder of February of 2016, Chad was angry. He had an attitude with everyone and not just me. He was mad at people at work, his family, his friends, and me. He was mad at his brother for having dogs and told him to get rid of them. He was so mad at the world it seemed. I didn't know why but I didn't read too much into it at the time. I just assumed he would get over it. A word of advice: don't ever assume someone will just "get over it."

Chapter 6:
The Blame Game

I have thoughts every day wondering why. I wonder if I would have said something different if it would have changed things. I constantly was playing the "what if" game. I blamed others and even blamed myself a lot. I have come to find out that is a normal part of the grieving process. However, in my situation, there will never be closure and there will never be an answer. He didn't leave a note and his phone was never found. I often think that I could have prevented his suicide that night, but I am a firm believer that it was inevitable and if it was not that night it would have been another.

When I first found out, I went back and forth with the thought that maybe he was murdered and maybe something wasn't right. I thought if he was murdered then I would not have to deal with so much guilt. Anyone that knew Chad though, knew he would not let another man shoot him with his own gun. Chad was shot in the back of the head and the exit wound came out above his left eye. No, that is not a normal place for someone to shoot themselves, but it is possible. I didn't see the scene and I didn't see any pictures. I talked to several deputies about the case and they indicated that there was no foul play involved.

No one had been there but Chad until the UTV drove up and found him. No foul play means that he was not murdered and the notorious "hitman" that was supposedly hired did not exist. I have made terrible decisions in my life, but I am not capable of that. I would never in my life think about killing another human being, let alone my husband. If I had wanted a divorce, I would have filed for divorce, plain and simple. I wonder who was just sitting around one day thinking about my life instead of their own and came up with that? I wonder why someone would do that? I lost my husband to suicide and if that is not bad enough, there were terrible people in the world who wanted to spread hate and judgment. Sad, sad, individuals.

For everyone that was so curious why Chad and I were even fighting or having issues with our relationship, our situation, as I discussed earlier, was alcohol. That was the barrier that kept us from having a successful marriage. We drank several times a week until intoxication. We surrounded ourselves with friends that drank and didn't do many things that did not require drinking. We drank because of so many unresolved issues in our lives that we were scared to talk about. We had talked about quitting again but never did. Any alcoholic knows what I am talking about. Selfish is the main word that comes to my head when I think about my alcoholism and my marriage. I was so selfish but at the same time, so was Chad. His brother told him that I needed help because my drinking was out of control. Chad needed to take care of himself before he could take care of me, though. Truth be told, we both should have been in a rehab facility, but that would have never happened because our egos were too big.

In a perfect world, I would still be married to a husband who was alive, living in our perfect little home, with our perfect little family. That is not my life. Every day, I wake up with a different perspective. One day I will be fine and positive and uplifting to others and other days, I do not want to get my head off the pillow and do anything. What happened to my life? Where did I go wrong? Why do I feel like everything in my life that could go wrong, has and still does? Why are people so full of hate and judgment? What happened?

I am the strangest person that I know and sometimes I wonder why my mind thinks and does what it does. I wonder why I can't get past this terrible tragedy that has occurred in my life and everyone else's? How have they gotten over it? How can I? Then, I remember that no one has gotten over it and no one ever will. The loss of Chad is an everlasting burden that will haunt us forever. What the heck was he thinking? Why would he do this to his family? His friends? He said a few days before he passed away that he never thought he would be good enough for "that" town. He would never be accepted because of his last name. A bias that was unnecessary. I told him otherwise but agreed to an extent. My last name was the reason I was unable to get a teaching job and ended up going a different route in life. We all know that it is all about who you know, unfortunately.

Mental illness is something that is not talked about and is something that is not discussed. Mental illness + substance use issues + lethal means is the recipe for suicide. I would always get mad during my training at my current job when they talked about warning signs. I argued the subject and told everyone that I had no warning signs. That's a lie. I tried to trick myself and make myself feel better by blocking out what had happened before Chad passed away. I was in denial for a very long time. The truth is, there were warning signs. There were signs that I should have noticed and paid more attention to. There were signs that I should have talked to him about and been a more empathetic and loving wife. Never in my life would I have imagined that Chad would have ended his own life.

I had a dream about Chad a few months after he passed away. He and I were sitting in the funeral home planning his funeral. He told me that he was glad that I didn't cremate him and asked me what took me so long to find him? I became angry and replied to him that I would have never expected him to be dead in a field somewhere.

I don't need other people telling me that the only reason Chad is dead, is because of me because I have struggled with it myself more than people will ever know. If it makes them sleep better at night, then they can think whatever they want. Their opinion means nothing to me. I remember telling people that we were fighting the night it happened and one of our deputies told me to stop telling people that because my story would get misconstrued. Of course, I was blamed and was all of a sudden sleeping with everyone within a 1,000-mile radius. The stories I would hear about myself were crazy. I still just want to know why everyone has been so intrigued by my trauma? The small town that we lived in wanted there to be more to the story. They wanted the juicy gossip about what happened and when they didn't get it, they made it up themselves to make it more interesting. Apparently, mental illness is not a good enough reason for someone to die by suicide.

Throughout the struggle, I have realized that the nonsense is normal. I have spoken to widows that had their husbands shoot themselves in front of them and they were blamed for doing it and making it look like a suicide. I have talked to widows who had their husband's family disown them and blame them for everything. I have been through extensive therapy since this event. I go off and on when I feel that I am struggling and need someone nonjudgmental to talk to. I told my therapist flat out that it was my fault. I told her what Chad had been through in his life and that I didn't make it any better. She told me that I could not blame myself for his past and could not blame myself for his actions. She is right. Ultimately and unfortunately, it was his decision. Should we blame the guy that I got the message from that night? Should we blame the guy he bought the gun from? Should we blame everyone because he felt alone and like he didn't have anyone to talk to? Should we blame "that" town because he felt he was never good enough? No. We can't place blame. None of us can. There are so many questions but there will never be an answer to those questions. You just have to carry the anger and the guilt until you are able to let go of it and not let it rule your life. You must let it go.

I didn't know that someone could be in such a dark place, even though they had the world at their fingertips. Even though they had a loving family, a successful career, and fantastic friends. I had been on anti-depressants since shortly after Charley was born. Chad and I had talked about him getting on medication because he was depressed but he never went. He would always just take my medication. He finally admitted to taking my medications. Why didn't I do something then? I didn't think depression could be that bad. I thought our drinking habits were normal. I never really thought about what went through my head when Chad would come home and tell me that he worked a suicide call or when I worked at the Sheriff's Office and had to deal with them. I have never really wondered why. I just always felt sad for their families. Chad would always say it was the "chicken shit" way out. How could someone do that to their children, he would say. Funny how life turns out, isn't it?

Did he take that easy way out? Did he do it to teach everyone a lesson? Who knows? The ignorance of some people, though. The ignorance of people that called themselves family and would not believe that he ever would do something like that and that I had to have something to do with it. If people think that he was not capable of doing it himself, then they are sadly mistaken. Everyone in this world is capable of it. Not only did Chad suffer from depression and a substance use issue, he had lethal means as I mentioned earlier. Chad was a people pleaser, which is not a bad thing, but in his case, it was. He was always out to help others because he was a genuinely good man. However, he was not superman and he was not a superhero. Chad was a flawed individual just like the rest of us are. We have good qualities and bad qualities. Chad did not deal well with abandonment, but I also wonder if he ever thought about how I would feel after dealing with being abandoned by not only my parents but him?

Chad made a comment when he was 10 years old that he wanted to get a knife, so he could just kill himself. Chad had made comments to several people that he was not going to go through another divorce and only seeing Charley every other weekend if I did leave him. Why did he think I was going to leave, you ask? As I mentioned earlier, I was selfish, and I treated him terribly. Just as he was selfish and treated me terribly. I took advantage of his loyalty and pretty much walked all over him at times. When Chad made those statements to people they didn't ever think that he would follow through with anything like that. They told me that. None of us want to believe that our loved ones are capable of anything like that, but we need to be prepared. We are all ticking time bombs. I know for a fact that Chad suffered from depression for a very long time and did not do anything about it. He wanted to go to marriage counseling and I always told him that I wanted to go by myself to get myself "right." I was so obsessed with saving money that I missed out on so many fun opportunities for Chad and me. I have a million regrets that I had to live with daily.

I think the main thing that I want everyone to know is that I survived. I barely survived, but I survived the nightmare that was and continues to be my life. I survived all of the gossip and slander that was spoken of me and my family. I survived people seeing me and whispering to others behind my back. I survived everything that everyone tried to do to bring me down. I pride myself on that. I am a strong woman and this situation has done nothing but make me stronger. Thank you to all of those who assisted in making me stronger!

If I can handle tragically losing my husband to suicide, then I can handle anything, absolutely anything, that this world throws at me. If I can handle people accusing me of being a murderer, then I can handle anything. To everyone who tried to bring me or my family down or even believed the hype, I would just like to say that you didn't win. You didn't get to us. We are stronger than you think, and we knew the true Chad Youngs. To everyone who placed blame on someone else for Chad's passing, please turn that finger around and ask yourself what you could have done to prevent this. Ask yourself what you can do to prevent someone that you love from doing the same thing.

Chapter 7:
Identity Crisis

When I married Chad on March 27th, 2010, Krystal Youngs became my new identity. I had lived a life of fun and excitement. I lived a life with someone who loved me and who was faithful to me. I lived a life with someone who had my back no matter what and who I was supposed to spend the rest of my life with. Our six years of marriage involved us going through me being pregnant with Charley and raising Charley until she was 4 years old. We went on small vacations and did what we could to have fun. Chad worked, I worked, and we took care of Charley when we were not working. Things were perfect; in some people's eyes. I have always said, and Chad always said that no one knows what goes on behind closed doors. No one really, truly knows someone unless they live with them and spend every day with them.

When Chad passed away, a piece of me did also. I was abandoned once again. I started to get a complex because I would see a pattern of abandonment throughout my whole entire life. I had no clue who I was or where I was going in life. I felt like Krystal Youngs was dead too. I couldn't remember Krystal Huff. I couldn't remember who she was or what she was like. I was Krystal Youngs but where was my Chad? Where was my Chad to complete our family? As I explained to Charley after it happened, Daddy was an angel in heaven and the brightest star in the sky. He is no longer with us but is always in our hearts.

I found myself clinging to everything that Chad was. Anything firefighter, EMT, or Lineman, I was all about. But who was I? Who was I without Chad? My mind did not know, and I did not know. I had no identity anymore.

I didn't know how to make life decisions without my husband. I didn't know how to do anything without my husband. Krystal Huff was independent and responsible, where was she? How come she did not step in? She was no longer either.

I was stuck in a crisis of identity. Much like the 100-other crisis' that I experienced after Chad's death. A crisis is defined as, "any rapid change or encounter that provides an individual with a "no exit" challenge, no choice but to alter his or her conduct in some manner." I had to alter my whole life and I had to alter my identity. After the course of a year and a half, I thought long and hard about it. I found that I still had an identity. I am Charley's mother, a widow, an author, a Community Support Specialist, a graduate student at Mizzou, a future social worker a granddaughter, a daughter, a niece, a cousin, an aunt, and even a great-granddaughter. I was still Krystal Youngs, I was just missing a significant piece of my life and had to learn to cope without that piece.

Krystal Youngs before Chad passed away was a pretty big, ugly mess. Throughout our marriage, I changed, and he changed. Chad changed, as he became complacent and did not do everything that he could have to make our family life running smoothly. He would come home from work and open a beer and sit on his phone all night. I was cooking, cleaning and taking care of our daughter and doing everything that needed to be done around the house. I changed from being a fun-loving, bright-spirited, kind and caring person into a resentful and bitter human being. My mind was a mess and so was I. I would talk badly about people and gossip about them and then be nice to their face. I would tell other people's secrets to others and then deny it when they called me out on it. I was selfish, and I wanted anything that would benefit me and make me look like a better person. I wanted people to like me and I wanted to be the "popular" one. I drank too much, and I left Chad at home, so I could go out and play softball with my friends and then go drinking at the bar and come home drunk.

I would go out to the bar to hang out for a "girl's night" and come home at 3 in the morning after driving my drunken friend to some random guy's house that she met at the bar. I was very attention seeking at this time in my life. I am not sure why because I had all the attention that I needed at home. I guess the "honeymoon" period had worn off. I was unhappy with life, I was unhappy with myself, I was unhappy with everything, but I put on a front.

I was also very attention seeking after Chad's death. If someone had a rule book on how to deal with men after being married for 6 years and newly widowed, I would have loved to read it. But, there is no rulebook and there are no rules. I wanted attention and as Chad always said, there will always be that one guy who will say all the right things at all the right times, but he is probably not the right one. Chad didn't want that to happen with me. It didn't until after he passed away. I was free, I was widowed and could do whatever I wanted. I had men texting and messaging me all the time that wanted to hang out and drink beer. They all had one thing in common also. They wanted to sleep with me, not just hang out with me and listen to me ramble. This was very difficult for me to deal with, but I did whatever my drunken mind thought was a smart idea at the time. I was dealing with my grief by being promiscuous and abusing alcohol to numb my feelings. I realized that I was coping with my issues the exact same way that my mother did when she experienced adversity in her life when she was a young girl. People didn't understand the trauma that my mind had just endured and that I was not thinking straight at all. I was not myself at all and I was just simply existing. I guess they thought I should have made all excellent decisions and be living a life of celibacy. I am laughing on the inside right now.

Do I think it was my fault? No. We could have worked anything out, but Chad chose not to work on it and to end his own life. I did not kill my husband. Today, I do not care to impress anyone or to make anyone think that I am better than I really am. Do I care about the rumors anymore? No. I am beyond that and beyond what people think they knew or know about me and Chad. No one in this world truly knows what happened except for Chad and the good Lord above, so for everyone still looking for an answer… you aren't going to find it. Time to move on and attempt to ruin someone else's life.

Krystal Youngs today thinks about others before she speaks or tries to. I have learned through my employment, going back to school and being involved in the church that I have no right to judge anyone in this world. Who cares what your house looks like or what you drive? Who cares about how you dress or how you do your makeup? Who am I to judge how someone else chooses to live their life?

Although my situation sucks, I do believe that I have become a better person throughout this learning process. I don't know if I could have gotten my head out of the bottle long enough before to actually find myself and realize who I was. I don't know if I could have gotten through this without leaving my last place of employment and the toxic friends that were left behind. They were left behind for a reason. They were not helping my situation at all. They were not helping me become a better person and had unreasonable expectations of a widow.

Today, my friends care about me for me. They don't care about what I wear, if my clothes are too tight, who I date, if I look a certain way or if I meet the criteria to be a part of their lives. They love me for me. They love me for me because they are truly good people and have taught me what a good person and a good friend really is. They make me happy and they appreciate me and my family for who we are. They know I am a basket case but still text me to make sure I am ok and to make sure that things are well with me when they cannot be around me. They even drive over to my house to make sure that I am ok in the middle of the night because they are worried about me.

After Chad's death, I only wanted one thing, not sympathy, but empathy. That is all I ever asked for. Someone to understand that my mind detached from my body after Chad died. My mind didn't know what the heck was going on and went wherever it needed to go to find satisfaction. I have come to realize that I do not need that satisfaction, but I need compassion and empathy from others. That is again why I always say that you don't know what someone is going through unless you have been through it yourself. I think after the trauma that I experienced that me going crazy and making terrible decisions in my life was to be expected. If people thought that I was just going to make great decisions and not be a basket case, then they were sadly mistaken. Those people do not understand what it is like to be in my situation and therefore, they don't understand the feelings and emotions that I have experienced. And I had no reason for feeling sorry for being sad all the time.

A lot of my identity crisis was made worse by my problem with alcohol. My continuous problem with alcohol did nothing for me but made me gain weight and make bad decisions. I don't blame my drinking entirely, but they are things that would have never happened had I not been drinking. I will not lie, but I was a huge mess. A mess in a way that goes back to finding satisfaction in my life and nothing else. All I wanted was the satisfaction and not a relationship. I wanted to be able to talk to whoever I want to whenever I wanted to and not be told I couldn't. I also lived in the opinions of others. I hated that but for a very long time, but I looked for the approval from others before I did anything in my life.

I am also a firm believer that real friends may not always agree with what you do but they will always be there for you and not turn their back on you.

Am I happy about how I treated Chad towards the end of his life? Absolutely not. It pains me to write about it, but it was the only way that I could really get the truth out and share my story. Guilt is a huge part of my life and forever will be. I know what I did wrong and what I should have done but there is no way to go back and change that. I just have to remember that if I ever get in another relationship to not make the same mistakes.

I have grown so much in two years and have learned some very hard life lessons. I have had to learn to deal with a lot of things that I shouldn't have had to until I was an old woman. I deal with it though, every single day. Every single day, I am expected to put on a smiley face and go about my day regardless of how sad and broken that I am on the inside. Nobody cared that I was sad and broken because after two years, I should be over it, right? I should be able to move on and never talk about Chad again in my life, right? Wrong! I will never move on and I will never stop being sad. The suicide of a spouse is something that just does not go away. You will think about it every single day. You will grieve every single day.

Chapter 8:
The Grieving Process

Denial: Chad wouldn't have done this. Chad had too much to live for. Chad always said he wouldn't do that.

Anger: What the heck were you thinking? How could you do this to your friends and family? I just want to throat punch you!

Bargaining: Maybe he didn't do this? Maybe someone else did? No, he did it, there is no evidence otherwise. But what if…?

Depression: I don't want to think, I don't want to move, I don't want to wake up. I want to stay in bed all day and do nothing but sulk in my sorrows. I hate my life. My life is terrible.

Acceptance: I know that Chad made the decision he did because he was depressed and didn't want to be a burden to everyone else. I accept his decision, even though it is hard to live with.

There are so many unanswered questions in life and so many questions that people feel they need the answer to, so they make up their own answer. The truth is, suicide is a major issue and not something that should be joked about. Anytime someone says, "He blew his head off" makes me so sad for them because of the hatred I see in them.

Suicide took my husband and ruined my life. Suicide turned me into a zombie for a long period of time and made me lose a ridiculous amount of weight. Suicide left my daughter and Chad's son without a father and me without a husband. Suicide broke me. Mental illness is a serious issue and something that affects many, many people, even if they fail to realize it or do not want to realize it.

Mental illness was behind Chad's death. It is not something that should be joked about or a reason to call someone "crazy" or "why don't you just go take your meds?" It is a serious disease that is overlooked and underfunded. When you pile substance use on top of mental illness, the receptors in your brain are messed up and you do not think rationally. Addiction makes you selfish, to begin with, and then adding mental illness to the mix can be fatal. Do I believe if Chad was not drinking that this wouldn't have happened? Absolutely. What can I do though? What if? Maybe if? That doesn't help either. The bargaining stage of grief is not pretty. No stage of grief is pretty, but you go back and forth and back and forth through each stage forever.

From my experience, grief has been a rollercoaster. Some days I am fine and function as a "normal" human being. Some days I am on the road and I bust out in tears after hearing "Amazing Grace" on the radio. You just never know when it is going to hit you and when you will turn into a basket case. Some days I don't want to live anymore and continuously hear voices in my head telling me that I am useless in life and deserve to be dead. You just have to learn to be prepared for whatever mood will strike you that day and you have to take it head on and work through the feelings. I can remember going through struggles a week at a time, two weeks at a time, and even a month at a time. I didn't want to talk to anyone or see anyone. I didn't want to go to work, but I had to.

Work is different for me though. No matter how upset or depressed that I am, I feel the need to help others. I don't care if I was having the worst day ever, I felt the need to get out and help my clients with their problems, as I felt they were more important than my own problems. I am human too and I am allowed to feel sad and most people should understand that.

Now don't get me wrong, sadness is not the only feeling associated with grief. I have been so angry some days that I had to control my anger before I hurt something or myself. I get angry at Chad for leaving me and his son and daughter all alone because he thought to relieve his pain, was more important than us. Nothing mattered to Chad at that time due to his mental state and being under the influence of alcohol. He wasn't thinking about anyone else's pain except his own. Why didn't he just go get help? Why didn't he talk to someone else? Why did he do this? What if Charley deals with adversity in the same way as her father and tries to die by suicide? We will never know and that is what kept me angry. Chad knew that he was suffering from depression and did not want to deal with the stigma surrounded by taking medication. He told me that himself. I did try to help him get the help he needed because I knew he was not himself. You can't help someone who isn't willing to help themselves first.

I am not an angry person however, I have turned into an angry person. I became very bitter after Chad died and blamed everyone else and failed to take a look at myself. I pretty much hated everyone in the following months after his death and felt as if no one was there for me, much like how Chad probably felt. People were there for me, but I never wanted to accept the help. During this time, I would go into work hungover, truth be told probably still intoxicated, and people just laughed at me like it was no big deal. No big deal, it was only Wednesday, and I decided to indulge in 45 margaritas the night before. No, I am not an alcoholic. I don't have a problem. This is the "norm." I felt like it was the "norm" but I also felt like no one cared. Here I was suffering the same addiction and the same sickness as Chad and no one cared. Except for one person, who mentioned before that he was the only one to reach out to Chad and me regarding our drinking problem.

I have made many terrible decisions and I regret each one of them. However, how do we learn? We don't give up. We keep moving forward and we learn from our mistakes. If we didn't make mistakes, even when we are 30, we will not learn. Our lives should consist of continuous learning to make each day better than the last. There is no right way to deal with grief. Each grief journey is unique. I feel that losing a loved one to suicide is especially hard when it comes to grieving. Simply because there will never be an answer. Your loved one took their own life and we will never know why or what we could have done to help them at that very time. We will never know what they were thinking about or why the demons were able to get the best of them.

Dealing with grief is the hardest part of the loss. You deal with it every single day and it never goes away. It doesn't get easier, you just know what to expect each reoccurring year and then you are able to cope with it a little bit better. Maybe. Is there a correct way to grieve? No. I struggled very much with being around people. I couldn't go to any events where there were a lot of people unless I was drinking. People would invite me over to hang out and I can't tell you the countless times I made an excuse just because I didn't want to leave my house. I barricaded myself and didn't want to deal with anything or anyone. Charley and I were just fine by ourselves. I never knew what mood I was going to be in, so I was scared to get myself in a situation that I couldn't get out of. I just wanted to be at home all the time.

Chad's father passed away 9 months after he did from bone cancer. Watching him die from this deteriorating disease was nothing worse than heartbreaking. However, this time I could tell my loved one that I loved them very much before he passed away, as I was unable to do that with Chad.

I would spend a lot of time in the field where Chad was when he took his own life when I finally got the courage to find out where it was. I would end up passing by it several times a week due to traveling for my work. Sometimes I would stop and pray. Sometimes I would stop and cuss at him. Sometimes I would just drive by and flip the bird. Every time I went to the spot, I was feeling a different emotion. It is still that way to this day. I never knew how it was going to affect me.

The anxiety was the worst. My heart would race, my palms would sweat, and my stomach would be in knots. Medication wasn't helping. Nothing was helping. I didn't know how to get over it because none of my coping skills were working for me. I tried deep breathing, I tried coloring, I tried everything. This landed me in therapy again. I had to talk to someone about what I was feeling and have validation that I was not insane. I needed reassurance because, in my mind, I was going insane. My therapist, of course, told me that my feelings and thoughts were valid and that I was grieving, not crazy.

One song on the radio, one show on tv, one word or phrase could cause me to go into a downward spiral. I just never knew. Anything could trigger or spark a memory that I had of Chad and cause more grief. We had so many good memories in our 9 years together and I found myself trying to grasp on to the good memories of us instead of the bad. I wanted to remember our relationship when we were so in love and happy. Not when we were both drunken monsters. How did I handle the grief? Honestly, it depended on the day. It depended on the thought and how I acted on it. Sometimes, I would go home and indulge in a 12 pack to continue to numb my pain with alcohol. I would then call people all night long and talk about life's problems in an attempt to ease my mind.

My mind was a scary place. I didn't want to be left alone in my own head or I think I seriously would have some major issues. My mind was messy, and I had to clear it up. I had to clear up the agony and the pain that I was experiencing in my life. It would turn out to be a continuous, never-ending battle. It would be a battle that I would never conquer.

 I received a phone call one day that my father had been hospitalized due to stomach pain. He had just been discharged from the hospital due to having a thickened gallbladder. For some reason, I knew this time, that something was not right, and I was right. His cancer had spread to his abdomen that was filling with cancerous fluid. He was 120 pounds and in pain. I went to the hospital to visit him and he told me he wanted to give up. He then asked me what I thought. I told him that I selfishly wanted him as long as I could, but if he was in that much pain, I did not want him to suffer. I spent the two-year anniversary of Chad's suicide with my father in the hospital. It kept me sober and sane and I was happy to be there. I usually have a get together at my house with all of Chad's close friends and relatives, but I was not feeling it this year. I did not want to be around people, as I knew I was about to endure another devastating loss in my life.

One day, my mother came to the hospital with me to see my father. I was secretly excited about this, as I had never had a conversation with both of them at the same time in my 30 years on this earth. It was fantastic. I heard stories of how they met, what they used to do for fun, the pets that they had (Abercrombie the cat), the cars that they drove and the drama that existed in their lives. It was very comforting for me to be able to hear these stories and realize that I, too, had a mother and a father, that loved me and cared for me, even though they did not raise me. I have repeatedly told both of them that I do not hold anything against them and I understand the cycle of addiction and what was going on in their lives at that time.

My father was sent home on hospice care and was still in a lot of pain. He liked to spend most of the time on his couch and watch Blue Bloods or those terrible car shows that Chad used to watch. I always thought, "Dad, you are a mechanic? You know everything about cars!" My stepmother always told me that he would wake up if she changed the channel and tried to watch something else.

One Monday, I received a call that they gave my father 24 hours to live. I got off work and headed down to the city. I would go down every day that week and enjoy every single moment I got to spend with my father. That Friday afternoon, I kissed my dad on the cheek. I said, "I am going home, dad. I love you very much and so does Charley Mae." He died that next Saturday morning at 6:28 am. I spent a week with my father and got to witness him flip people off, tell them they were going to hell, and asking why he was not dead yet. The only thing that he would tell me was, "I love you."

The day he passed, I went to his house and saw his lifeless body on the couch. I sat next to him and cried, and the grief process started all over again. I was devastated that I lost another important man in my life. I asked my father before he passed if he would beat the crap out of Chad for me when he got to heaven and he said he would hunt him down first thing. I knew that Chad was going to get a run for his money!

I spoke at my father's celebration of life. This was the first time that I had ever admitted to having an addiction. I admitted it in front of a room of several hundred people. I was so nervous, but I felt compelled to speak and let everyone know what a great person my father was regardless of his past. I had to stand in that dreaded line again and hug everyone and feel like I had to bathe in germ-x when I was done. However, I was so happy to hear all of the wonderful things about my father and all of the lives that he had personally changed. So many men told me that my father changed their lives and contributed to their sobriety.

I again struggled with my sobriety during this time. I asked my father for one thing that was very special to him, his 11-year AA coin. He not only left me his coin, but his whole AA book, coffee stains, highlighter marks and all. He wrote in the front of it, "Krystal, I love you. Dad." It was the best thing that he could have ever left me. He also left me a Snap-on jacket, like the one he had given Chad that he was wearing when he shot himself. He told me to remember that every time I wore it that it was him giving me a hug. I still, to this day, wear the jacket, even if it is 80 degrees outside. I was more prepared this time, but I felt like my grief was just compiling upon my previous grief. It did not make it any easier. I learned that regardless of whether it was an expected death or unexpected death, all death still hurts the same.

Chapter 9:
Widow

I won't lie to you. I always hated the word "widow." I felt like I was supposed to be some old lady with 50 million cats, a black veil, and no life. I didn't want to be labeled a widow. I didn't even like to change my Facebook status to widowed because it hurt too bad. It was another reminder that I was robbed of my future.

Unless you are a widow/widower, you will not understand the journey that we go through. It is not the same as if you are divorced, if your dog died or if your great aunt Sally died. A word of advice, please stop comparing your loss to those of a widow or widower. It is not the same.

When I first became a widow, I did not eat anything for several weeks. I was so high on Klonopin that I had no idea what was going on around me. I wasn't hungry, and I was only just existing. After everyone was done feeling sorry for me and had stopped contacting me, the alcohol came back out. You could say that most of my grieving was done while drinking away my past sorrows. I thought I could drink all my feelings away and everything would be all better. Obviously, that did not happen.

I hated going to the doctor or the dentist and having them ask for my emergency contact. You must then, again explain that you need to change it, most likely to someone who won't be there when you need them because your last emergency contact is now dead. I hated having to call every single company that he had and account with and having to explain that he was dead. And, NO, I do not want to put it in my name. I hated getting the phone calls two years after his death having to say that he was deceased.

The number of times that I had to scan and send that damn death certificate was ridiculous. As well as the wonderful autopsy report and police report. It broke me when I had to read those. I was so happy to be able to lock them up and not see them anymore. As his death was undetermined, I would have to fight with life insurance companies who didn't want to pay out. I would have to deal with evil people stating that I was not "deserving" of my husband's retirement account and having $70k of my husband's money basically stolen. Death really does bring out the true colors in everyone. You really do find out who has your back and who does not.

You are expected to do so much even though your brain is fogged over (this is called "widow brain"), and you have no idea what the heck you are doing. Chad did so much for me in my life and I didn't have any of his help anymore. I was never in my life late on paying a bill until I was a widow. There was no one to change my oil, clean the drains, fix sheetrock, mow and weed eat the yard, teach Charley how to run a drill, no one. I am pretty sure that it was a good 6 months after Chad passed away before I actually got an oil change in my car. I was forced to be the independent Krystal that I always claimed to be. Chad would always rip the top of the oil filter carton and write on it the mileage for my next oil change. He would also include an "I love you" or "you are the best wife ever" on it. I would weep when I found those in my glove box.

I often used the "widow card." This is the card that widows use to get what they want. I used it at a Luke Bryan concert by making a sign that said, "I am a widow and I need a hug." Unfortunately, I didn't get a hug, but he did touch my hand. And yes, I have washed it since then, even though I didn't want to. I used the widow card to con my coworkers into bringing me morel mushrooms to work, into getting scholarships, having people mow my yard, etc. I used it to manipulate others in a sense.

My coping skills since becoming a widow have been both positive and negative. My number one coping skill was negative and that was alcohol. Other negative coping skills included promiscuity, using others, and binge eating. I used to be 110 pounds and that quickly got back up to 150. I used every diet in the book, but my regular alcohol consumption kept the weight on. Yes, I developed a female beer belly and I was not proud of it. I would experience a "mid-life crisis," as I referred to it also. This included getting a nose piercing and three tattoos (more to come I am sure). Chad hated tattoos, so a week after he passed, I had his name tattooed on my back. Now he is stuck with me forever! I would also become angry at my Pontiac G6 for the air conditioner quitting so I said screw it and bought a newer car, so I didn't have to deal with it. I drive all day and don't have time to take a car to a shop so getting a more reliable one sounded like a better plan to me.

I did exhibit some positive coping skills. I started planting flowers and trying to make my house look nice. I started to do things around the house to make it look better and keep it clean. I started doing more with Charley and started taking her places where we could bond and do fun things together. I would also grief shop. Yes, I shopped a lot and Amazon Prime became my best friend. I know that Chad is in heaven cussing me because I used to get on to him for spending money and today, I spend it like there is no tomorrow. You can't take it with you when you die, right? So, why not spend it now?

I am not a very festive person. Chad was the Christmas freak that loved everything about Christmas and I would be in the corner shouting, "Ba humbug." The cycle continued after he died, and I was still a scrooge. I would still decorate and do all the gifts but on the inside, I was broken. I would rather have been propped up on a bar stool playing Keno than spending Christmas with anyone. I would open the Christmas totes and find my husband and his ex-wife's matching stockings and Christmas ornaments that would quickly end up in my fire pit. I would still put up his Dale Earnhardt Jr. stocking with ours but wouldn't ever decide what I could get him for Christmas, so I usually filled it with candy and then ate it myself.

When do you take off your ring? Everyone is different. I took mine off about a year and a half into it. I would still wear it out sometimes in an attempt to scare men off, as most men didn't want anything to do with a married woman. I would often go to the bar without it and sob to young 23-year-old boys that I was a poor, poor, sad widow. We would then drive around, and they would drop me off and ask me if I owned my home or rented. I would become angry and yell, "Of course I own my home, I am 30 years old and have a life!" That would quickly scare them off and they wouldn't ever contact me again.

Two years into widowhood, I joined a group on Facebook called Widow Dark Thirty. Being in the group made me feel a sense of normalcy and made me feel like people really understood me and could relate to my situation. I read a book by Michelle Miller called *"Boys, Booze, and Bathroom Floors"* and I for once felt a sense of peace. I felt like all the haters in the world had no idea what a young grieving widow goes through and that I was normal. My feelings and emotions were normal, and my actions were normal. They were one of a young grieving widow trying to get her life back together. It is very hard to pick up and function after you lose half of your life. Especially when you are left to raise your child on your own with no guidance and no help. Michelle Miller has been such an inspiration to me. Her second book, *"Vodka Soup for the Widowed Soul: Stories of Grief, Alcohol, Infidelity, Cursing, and Hope"* was also very inspiring to me. I could relate to a lot of the things that she discussed and again, I felt a sense of peace. I highly recommend that you make those books your next Amazon purchase.

I also read a book called *"Widowed. Rants, Raves, and Randoms"* by John Polo, Better Not Bitter Widower. This book gave me a look at another side of grief and tremendously helped me realize that I was not crazy, as I had once thought. There is a section in his book called Sit Down. And Shut up. It talks about how people do not understand what it is like to be widowed and the best thing to do is just… sit down and shut up. You can't snuggle up next to your husband/wife and judge a widow for doing something that you think is wrong. Sorry! John Polo says it how it is, which makes it a very enjoyable read.

I developed a hate for adulting once again. I hated having to put in an ice maker by myself, change the riding lawn mower battery by myself, changing my car headlights by myself, learning to put in weed eater string by myself, among all the other things that I would have to do myself. Could I have asked for help? Yes, and I did sometimes but I wanted to show myself that I could be independent, and I could make it on my own without him. I didn't want to be grieving and sad for the rest of my life. I wanted to get back out there and do what I needed to do to survive on my own.

I learned that time does not heal anything but instead makes it more real. Time did not heal anything in my life. Adversities kept arising in my life and kept slapping me in the face. Adversities kept testing me and made me want to just quit. Did I? Absolutely not. I was bound and determined that nothing was going to bring me down. Nothing was going to come between me and my daughter and I would not let her down. I did not want her to grow up without both of her parents and I made sure that didn't happen. I will break the cycle.

Being a widowed parent is less than desirable also. There were nights that Charley and I would eat cookies and milk for supper because I am an awesome parent and if that's what she wanted then that's what she got. I maybe even let her eat Fruit Roll-Ups before school because I was convinced they contained real fruit. I let her wear makeup in First Grade. If me letting Charley wear makeup in First Grade is the most rebellious thing that she does, then I have succeeded as a parent.

Charley was very self-sufficient, and I often took advantage of that. I would be on the phone and she would paint her whole face with my lipstick, take a knife to the couch, make scrambled eggs in an aluminum bowl in the microwave, or try to make her own slime. I would get off the phone and be surprised by her antics and new creations. Have I failed as a mother? Probably. I am happy to say though that my daughter received "Bucket Filler of the Month" at school her first month of Kindergarten and First Grade and "Bucket Filler of the Year" in Kindergarten. I took that as a "mom score." I was doing something right. Yay me!

I always had people tell me that I was being too lenient and that she was walking all over me. Again, I stopped caring what others said to me. She was my daughter and I was going to raise her however I wanted to. The poor girl had to go through one of the worst possible traumatic experiences in her life at four years old. I am not going to caudle her, but I am not going to let her let people walk all over her either. Today, she will tell you herself that she is a "ninja." As for me, I am a "ninja widow!"

Being a young widow is a unique experience. You must deal with so many trials and tribulations. You must deal with the judgment of everyone and everyone watching every single move you make. Most of the time, you probably didn't make that move but someone thought it would be funny if you did so they started a rumor. Again, everyone wants their juicy widow gossip! I got tired of being judged so I stopped judging others. It didn't stop them from judging me, but it made my life a heck of a lot less dramatic. I got rid of the toxicity in my life and decided that it was time for me to be happy.

Being a widow sounds like great fun, right? Yeah, that's what I thought. Although I would do anything to have Chad back, this is the new me. I have to label myself a widow and will forever be a widow no matter what. Remarrying is the last thing that ever comes to my mind, although some days I am certain that I would like to settle down with my second Mr. Right and live a fun life again. I often argued with myself on whether or not I wanted to date someone like Chad or someone completely different than Chad. I would silently judge others and pick out every single flaw that I could just because I knew that I was not ready to be dating again.

I never understood how dating was so easy when I was a teenager. Nobody cared about who I dated, and nobody really cared about my life at all. Now that I am a widow, it is almost like you are your own celebrity because everyone is watching your every move and so quick to call, text, or Facebook message whoever they think will actually care. I had my own "widow paparazzi." I often wondered what they gained from stalking me so much. Did they think that it would affect Chad in any way? Were they going to go running to him and tell him that I was with someone else? No. They were just plain stupid.

Dating at 30 years old was a whole different ballgame. Instead of the whole, "you are cute, let's go out" dating, it had turned into, "do you have a 401k?" or "where do you see yourself in 10 years?" dating. It was just different because I was different. I had a different identity than I had before. I would get angry with others who took their relationships for granted and not realize what they have. I wish I could argue with my husband again! The single, widowed life was not at all what I wanted for myself at 30 years old. But, like everything else I have experienced and learned, you just do what makes you happy.

There are so many things that suck once you become a widow. You are sleep deprived, you are broke, you are tired, and you are just miserable. You try to think of things that will make you feel better and then you end up writing a book that you think might help you. You pretty much lose your mind, but you are able to keep it together…. someway and somehow, you just do.

Chapter 10:
Moving Forward

There is no such thing as a book for widows to explain to us how to move forward and live our lives. Yet again, another period in your life that you are going to be judged no matter what you decide to do. Whether your marriage was perfect or terrible, you will always be judged. Whether you decided to date 2 days or 2 years later, you will be judged either way. People don't think about what is going on with another person before they place their unneeded judgment. The grief clichés did nothing but make me mad. I know people just wanted to be nice, but you will never truly understand someone's situation unless it has happened to you. I do not believe that everything happens for a reason and I do not believe that it was a part of my plan. I believe it was a crappy situation that I am forced to deal with.

My bad decisions after Chad's death led me to make a number of terrible mistakes. My plans for sobriety were long gone, obviously. I still felt like I needed someone, though. There was one blessing in disguise that came out of one of my bad decisions. A blessing that did me so much good. I found out who my true friends were. I found out that if someone is going to judge me due to who I choose to hang out with then they aren't really my friend anyway. I had friends that still stuck by me. I had friends tell me that I was an awful person because "Chad's body was not even decomposed yet" and I wanted to date. I cannot make this stuff up. Like I had mentioned before, 2 days or 2 years, I would still be judged.

Moving forward includes not caring about what other people think about you. A question that I am often asked by friends, clients, family, etc. is how to not care about what other people think of you. I believe this is a common issue for a lot of individuals and can be very tricky to overcome depending on your personality and belief systems.

Why do people care so much about what other people think? Do they need reassurance? Do they want everyone to like them? I can say that I did for a very long-time care about what others thought of me and would be hurt and broken whenever I would hear that someone was spreading hate about me. I would try to argue and justify my actions with that person and it would get me nowhere but being bitter, resentful and angry at myself. I don't have to justify my acts to anyone. Especially people that aren't a part of my life. Many people decide to share their negative opinions about me, not to me, but to people that I am close to because they know it will get back to me. Why? Are they scared of how I will react to them if they said it to my face? Or maybe it is the fact that it could possibly be a lie, but it brings much more joy to people's lives to gossip and spread around lies than to confront the person that the gossip was about.

I am going to share a few things with you to maybe help you to overcome what others think of you.

1. Someone who speaks negatively about your life is possibly dealing with their own demons.

This relates to bullying as well. We all know that the "bully" at school is usually the kid who has a dysfunctional home life and is looking for a way to act on their emotions. They do it the wrong way though. Making someone else's life miserable is not going to make your life any better. I find it sad that others are so fixated on bringing other people down instead of building themselves up. It is unfortunate for them, worrying about someone else's life instead of their own is their main concern. When what someone else says about you starts affecting you then you are letting them win. You are letting them get the satisfaction of knowing that their nonsense affected your life in a negative way. That is exactly what they are looking for. Don't give it to them. Instead, offer them an ear and be kind. Pray for them and that one day they will be able to find peace and joy in their lives.

2. You can't please everyone.

I have learned in my 30 years on this earth that not everyone is going to like me. Some people won't like what I am about, some people won't like what I wear, some people won't like blah, blah, blah. Since when is it your job to please everyone? Who has time for that anyway? I know I do not. At one point in my life, I felt the need to be accepted by everyone, however that quickly changed. Being a widow, especially, everyone has their own perception of how they think a widow should act and behave. As I have always said though, you don't know my journey unless you have walked in my shoes. So that perception that everyone else has…means nothing to me. I am continually changing. I am continually making mistakes and learning from them and so is everyone else. Our mistakes belong to us and no one else.

3. Be true to you.

You know who you are, and you know what makes you happy. So… do it! Do what makes you happy and don't worry about what the next man thinks. Now, I will say that it is good to have a few opinions that you very much cherish in your life to help you make sure that you haven't fallen off of your rocker but other than that, it is your life so do what you want. Death is inevitable, so why not make the most of the time we have on earth? Take care of yourself, get your nails done, get your hair colored, exercise, go on a trip, go on a date. Do something that is going to make you feel good. Always practice self-care to eliminate a burn out in your life.

4. Analyze the situation.

I have heard some of the most hilarious stories about myself. Some that were so farfetched that I often wonder who was dumb enough to come up with something like that. I think the day after my husband passed away, people were already pointing fingers and sharing their opinion of what they thought the real story was. I continue to hear these made-up scenarios to this day and it has almost been 2 years. One day, after I had heard that someone drove by my house and saw me and my brother in law through the blinds, I just laughed. It was all that I could do. No need to justify, no need to speak my peace, I knew that someone just came up with that in their head to justify my husband's death to appease their own little mind. Good for them, I got a good laugh out of it. I thought to myself how this really affected my life. It didn't. It didn't affect my life at all. I thought to myself that no one can bring me down and more importantly no one's words can bring me down. People have opinions and that is great. Unless people are really willing to sit and listen, it is a waste of time trying to argue or explain yourself to anyone. So, what do you do?

Laugh and move on. Just because someone doesn't like something about you or thinks you did something in the past has no bearings on you or your future. So, I say to you, get out and live. Get out and do what makes you happy regardless of what anyone else thinks.

Moving forward was not only about relationships, it was about everyday life and how to run a household by myself. It would be about how to survive off one income and make a decent living for my daughter and me. It involved me going through nightmare after nightmare with insurance companies, credit card companies, mortgage companies, retirement companies, and everybody constantly needing some sort of paperwork. It would be a year after Chad's death until I could finally put away his death certificate, autopsy report, and police report and keep it put away.

Moving forward in terms of my mental state has been a roller coaster. From me contemplating suicide myself, to me learning to live and cope with adversity, I have been through it all. Sometimes, my mind can switch in an hour, a day, a week or a month. That also would depend on how much alcohol I had consumed. After Chad's father passed away, 9 months after Chad did, I hit another rock bottom. I was drinking heavily again and one Friday night I laid in the middle of my living room on the floor, planning my suicide. I didn't want to live anymore, and I didn't want to deal with anything. I was to that stage and the demons were trying to get the best of me and almost did. I laid on the floor bawling and trying to write a suicide note at the same time. Charley was asleep and was unaware that her mother was such a disaster, or I know she would have been trying to console me.

A picture of Charley fell from my end table and landed next to me on the floor where I was laying. How? Why? I believe that was my sign from God to buck up and keep going. He was telling me not to give up. I didn't, and I kept going. Moving forward has not been easy, as you can see. It has been the hardest thing ever. I would go through several days of hearing the demons and experiencing panic attacks. I would have to pull over while driving down the road because my vision would get blurry and all I could hear was everything bad that everyone has ever said about me. There were several times that I was ready to be with Chad and say screw everyone else. I then understood what Chad was going through.

My moving forward involved me writing this book for closure. It involves me telling the world what it is like to be a survivor and how to persevere the grief and adversity that you will be susceptible to, healthy or unhealthy, it is your choice. I want people to realize that even though you were dealt a bad hand at life, you can still be a functional adult. You can still get up, go to work and live your life with a huge hole in your heart. It is possible, I know because I am doing it right now. When I refer to moving forward, it does not involve me ever forgetting about Chad. I will never forget about Chad. Never. He will forever be a part of my life until I cross over to the other side and am with him.

Does life suck some days? Absolutely! Do I feel like I continually fail at many areas of my life? Absolutely! Do I wonder day to day how I am going to survive my grief? Absolutely! When someone dies by suicide there are so many unanswered questions, and nobody knows why.

Blame is placed, and people are downright awful. No matter what happened between Chad and I and no matter what happened that dreadful night that I will never forget, it is not going to change the fact that he is not coming back. If people want to blame me and say, "How can you even talk to her?" to my friends then that is absolutely fine. I would say to those people like I say to a lot of people; Try to walk a mile in my shoes and see how you would survive. There are liars, cheaters, and haters all over this world and if someone wants to tell me that they are perfect then good for them. I was not perfect. I am not perfect. Although, I am not to blame. It is possible to move forward with life even though you don't want to and don't feel like you ever can.

My final words to everyone who blamed me, to all the people who gave up on me, and to all the people who felt the need to spread gossip about Chad's situation, shame on you. Shame on you for thinking that you were better than Chad or me and that your life was better than ours. Shame on you for not having compassion and empathy for Chad or his family after he passed away and instead spread lies and hate in the community. It was utterly disgusting the things that people decided to spread around and they didn't even know the truth. Regardless of the anger, hate and bitterness that Chad's situation has caused me, I have given it to God. I gave all my anxieties to Him in hopes that I will find some peace and hope in my life. I have found peace, hope and joy in this world that is full of hate, anger, gossip, and rage. And there is nothing anyone can do about it.

I am a survivor. I pray for the people who have let me down and hurt me and my family. I forgive them no matter how hard it is for me. We need love and compassion in this world, not hate and discontent. I am deeply saddened, that it took this big of a situation to make me realize that I needed help. I never wanted my life to be like this, no one would.

I will have to learn the correct ways to cope with my emotions each and every day. I will make mistakes and I will fail but I will always get back up and keep moving forward. Chad will forever be a part of my life and in my heart. I will do whatever I can to keep his memory alive. Charley will never be able to forget how wonderful her father was. Chad was a wonderful soul, gone way too soon. He will be forever loved and forever missed. Remember, you never move on, you just move forward. Love one another and be kind. You never know when your last day or your loved one's last day will be.

Conclusion

Life is a complicated journey, especially when you are grieving every single day. I have learned that even though I was dealt a terrible deck of cards at the beginning of my life and at 30 years old, I cannot give up hope. I am always striving to get better and truly believe that the cycle can be broken, and addiction can be overcome. Many times, individuals give up hope and start to go down a dark, scary road of depression. Living with anxiety and depression every day is not a fun thing but with some self-care and coping skills, it is manageable. I didn't ask to be a grieving widow at 28 years old, left to raise our 4-year-old daughter on my own. It was the life that was chosen for me and I have been forced to live it. I can honestly say that I have tried to make the most of my life since the passing of Chad. I am venturing out and getting out of my comfort zone and I love doing it. I am truly blessed in my life, regardless of the past adversity that I have endured.

Throughout my life, I realized that I dealt with life the same way my parents did, even though they did not raise me. There are similarities in my story, my mother's story, and my father's story. The adversity, addiction and the abandonment that I faced throughout my life have been terrible and excruciatingly painful. I survived, however, it has not been easy, and it has not been a walk in the park. It has been the hardest, most agonizing thing that I would ever have to experience. My life was spent feeling less than and like I was unworthy, but I was still able to push through and be successful. Successful in a way that I did everything that I was supposed to do in life and in the right order.

Today, I understand the struggle. I understand what my mother and father were going through. I do not fault either one of them on what happened when I was growing up and they both know that. I love them both and again, am grateful for the time that I got to spend with my father, especially before he passed away. I am grateful for the time that I currently get to spend with my mother and my stepfather.

My grandparents still support me and love me every single day. They may not always agree with my decisions (the tattoos and piercings), but they love me through them. They have watched me grow into the human being that I am today and know that they contributed to my successes.

Today, I am working on my Master's Degree in Social Work. I am working towards becoming more educated to bring awareness to suicide prevention and intervention. America's adolescent population needs to be educated on suicide and mental health issues and we need to work to eliminate the stigma of suicide and mental illness. This is where we come into play and need to educate others and help others that are having a rough time and need a friend.

I am no better than anyone else and do not act that way. I do not judge others on their past or what they choose to do with their future. I love all my friends and family the same regardless of what they choose to do because that is who I am today.

Quotes from Friends and Family of Chad A. Youngs

"Chad was such a loving, helpful individual. He was an individual who never made you feel like you were being judged by him. He would always smile and speak when he saw you. I will always remember him and his helpfulness to me with Christmas Around the Square and the Nativity scene, (that was and is always having issues with its lights staying on). He would come at the drop of a hat to help me. He was one of kind and I am so thankful and blessed to have known Chad." – Sally Black

"Chad was a great young man that brought much happiness and joy to a beautiful young lady that consider my adopted daughter even though she is not my daughter or adopted. Everyone should have the opportunity to meet the love of their life. I am thankful to have known Chad if even briefly." -Jeff Ellis

"He made me laugh sometimes in dispatch so hard that it hurt!!! He would always make you happy,"- Jackie Parker

"When Chad met your Great Grandmother Minnie for the first time, he saw she was having some difficulty walking. He made a point to find a walker and bring it back to her, which she used the entire visit. It was so kind of him."- Jennifer Monson

"Krystal, my fond memory of Chad was how he stepped up after I lost my husband. He made sure that I was doing alright and was always offering to help me with anything I needed. He would call me stop by to check on me, and even brought me some flowers to cheer me up. I'll never forget when I told Chad that he and I were related, he gave me that sweet grin that I'll never forget and said, "you don't want too many people to know you're related to me, you might lose a lot of friends." We both got a big laugh out of that one. I'll always have a special place in my heart for Chad, his kindness during my time of needing a friend will always be remembered. I love that young man as one of my own." – Linda Lollar

"As for anyone, it was a shock to hear about Chad's passing. He was always a joy to hear from and talk to. I worked for the city of Gallatin for 15 years and for the last 6 years, spent a lot of time with Chad right beside me. We worked on water main breaks in the hottest, and the coldest of weather worked power outages in some of the most severe thunderstorms.

I remember right before he started working for the city seeing him working at John's, changing and repairing tires. When Roger Loxterman said he was coming to work for the City, I knew he would fit right in. He was always wanting to learn more, and I was more than willing to teach him. He took right off, sometimes to a point that he was hard to keep up with. He was never afraid to jump right in, even when the mud was up to his waist.

I remember not long after he started with the city, he was reading meters, which was his first job, and he walked by the bucket truck I was working out of, to put a new fuse in a transformer. Chad asked if he could ride up in the bucket with me and I let him. He was hooked on it and wanted to work in the electric department. When an opening arrived, just as Chad was, he jumped right in. He loved trimming trees and working power outages. We had a saying at the time, "We live for thunderstorms." Because it was always a thrill and a little bit of danger.

I remember how at times, you never knew what to expect from Chad. There was a time that we were changing a meter at Dr. Irby's residence. The valve broke while we were working it and water was shooting in the air. It was a hot summer day, so getting wet didn't bother him much. I ran back to the plant to get the parts we needed and came back to find Chad and Natasha Irby (who was 5 or 6 at the time) playing in the water that was spraying in the air.

I remember going to power outages and Chad would have a young Bryce with him, strap him in the bucket truck and go with me for the repair in the middle of the night. There were times that I was glad that Chad was an EMT, like when we were taking down some Christmas decorations in on a cold January, I stayed in the bucket too long and when I came down, I went unconscious. Chad took care of me till we got to Dr. Dickinson's office.

I just wanted to say that I did enjoy working with Chad during those years. There were times that he made me so mad that I thought we were going to blows, but we always remembered that our jobs meant we had to depend on each other and we remained friends. I did not mention earlier that when Lisa and I were looking at getting into the rental house business, Chad was our first renter. Had we had more like him, we probably would still be in business.

I could go on and on with more memories of working with Chad. Like when I was digging a hole by the wastewater plant with the backhoe, he wanted to know if he could try it. I think if I would have let him, he would have dug to

China. That was Chad, most of the time he made work fun. He was always willing to help. If you needed him, he would be there.

The Sunday before his passing was the last time we spoke. We spoke on the phone and just about everything going on, the city, Krystal, Charley, and Bryce. It was a very enjoyable conversation. I just about fell out of my chair when Lisa told me about his passing. Chad was the last member of the City utility crew from when I was there. He will be greatly missed by so many. I believe the reason we talked the Sunday before his passing was that I just missed working with him. I wish I had employees like him where I'm at now. But Gallatin only had one. I would have never thought that that would have been the last time I heard his voice. I still miss working with you, Chad." - Steve Reid

"Beautiful heart, gentle loving soul." Lori-Ann Latimer

"He told me a story about the "claw toy machines". He said "that's why I have trust issues." – Jenny Youtsey

"I did not know Chad well, but what I did know of the man was that he was a person I did want to know better. My time with Chad was short but so very valuable. I met Chad and his fellow Gallatin Firefighters at a fire class in Cameron I assisted with one day a week for 4 hours, approximately 6-7 months long. I looked forward to seeing the people in the class. Most times, I dreaded being away from my family, but not that night. I shared a bond with that class and especially the men from the Gallatin Fire Department. Chad, Doug, Darren, Kyle and Jason were in a league of their own. Their knowledge, skill, character, with and enjoyment made them stand out in a crowd. We had a lot of good times in our short venture together. I had always hope to work alongside them one day. That would truly had been an honor. When I think specifically of Chad, I remember his smile and work ethic. A proud father whose eyes lit up like fireworks when it came time to do the "dirty work." Being a firefighter was important to Chad and he lived to high standards because of the work that he did. I will continue to pray for Chad, his family, and the Gallatin Fire Department with these trying times. Thank you for sharing Chad with me as I am a better man through my time with him. God Bless You. With deepest sympathy and respect." -Jamey McVicker

"CHAD, I love you, brother." - Brandi Cox

"Always had a smile on his face no matter what was going on. He had a heart of gold." -Lynette Kaneer

"Chad—Caring, handsome, amazing, determined and my best friend. It has been two years now and I am still hoping to get a phone call or surprise visit from you and your beautiful family. You are a great guy that will do anything for anyone of your friends and for that I hope to one day be like you. And you go far beyond that for your family. My world will never be the same without you in it, you have left a gigantic hole. On my darkest days, I look for your smile to light me up just like you do when you walk in a room. You are larger than life and you will never be forgotten! Not even this can tear you away from me, my best friend. There will never be a replacement for my birthday adventures. Love you Spongebob, aka The Chad." – Margie Barlow

Acknowledgements

My sister, Brandi, I love you so much. You have gone through this lifelong journey with me. We haven't always gotten along but never forget that I love you and always will. You are stuck with me forever.

To Chad's "work wife," Eric Kloepping, thank you. You have been there for me more than you will ever know. You have always made sure I was ok and always kept Charley and I a part of your life. Chad is looking down on you and is probably feeling sorry for you for having to put up with me so much, but I know he is very thankful for you.

Little Brother, Jason, you were the only one who really recognized our struggle. You were the only one that tried to intervene. You have always been there for me through the thick and thin on this journey of grief. We have each other's backs and we have a bond that will never be broken. I love you, brother!

To my family and friends who are there for me always and loved me unconditionally…. I love you more! I thank you all so much for being there for me through the toughest times in my life and helping me strive to be a better person. Without all of you, I would not be who I am today. Thank you. To everyone who stuck with me through the adversity, thank you. I will forever cherish your nonjudgmental and loving souls.

* Co-Author Credit: Jason Youngs

*Photo Credit: Nikki Berry Photography – Gallatin, Missouri.

IN LOVING MEMORY

Chad Alan Youngs

April 25, 1978- February 28, 2016

IN LOVING MEMORY

Roy Michael Decha

March 17, 1965-March 24, 2018

IN LOVING MEMORY

Daniel Charles Youngs

July 24, 1954- November 30, 2016

Made in United States
North Haven, CT
26 April 2023

35900052R00072